W9-ASA-302

Dynamic
Change and
the Urban
Ghetto

Dynamic Change and the Urban Ghetto

Alan Walter Steiss
Virginia Polytechnic Institute
and State University

John W. Dickey
Virginia Polytechnic Institute
and State University

Bruce Phelps
Mid-Willamette Valley Council
of Governments

Michael Harvey
C & P Telephone Company

Lexington Books
D.C. Heath and Company
Lexington, Massachusetts
Toronto   London

Library of Congress Cataloging in Publication Data
Main entry under title:

Dynamic change and the urban ghetto.

    1. Social change. 2. Sociology, Urban.
3. Sociology—Methodology. I. Steiss, Alan Walter.
HM101.D97   301.24'09173'2   74–14409
ISBN 0–669–96073–x

Published simultaneously in Canada.

Printed in the United States of America.

International Standard Book Number: 0–669–96073–x

Library of Congress Catalog Card Number: 74–14409

Contents

List of Figures

List of Tables

**Dynamic
Change and
the Urban
Ghetto**

1
Social Change in Urban Society

As Washburne has observed, change is so built into the social structure of modern society that it has become accepted as one of the normal expectations of life.[1] While change is an ubiquitous characteristic of our urban society, it would be fallacious to view it as an epiphenomenon, involving the orderly transition from one stable, integral phase of human behavior to another. The effects of social change impact various segments of society differently; the ability of social groups to adapt to changing conditions in modern society is not a constant, but a significant variable. To plan for growth and change requires that consideration be given to the nature of change itself, and to the motivations and consequences of individual and aggregate acts that give rise to (or serve as obstacles to) social change. It is necessary to examine the direction and pace of change, the dynamic equilibrium between change and continuity, and the leverage factors that presumably can be manipulated to bring about more orderly planned changes. While classic studies have focused on the nature and mechanisms of social change at the societal level, only recently have parallel studies been initiated regarding the consequences of change for segments of a given society.

The purpose and intent of this book is to examine the implications of social change for one important segment of modern society—the urban ghetto. To accomplish this objective, a simulation model has been developed to examine the individual and aggregate behavior of three key social variables—education, health, and income—over time. As used here, a simulation model is one that duplicates the observed conditions of reality through predetermined and consistent rules for handling and manipulating data. It typically treats society—or that part of society under consideration—as a system of interacting variables that react to data introduced into the system externally. The basic format, conceptual framework, and programming techniques of this model are derived from the work of Forrester on the structure and dynamics of systems.[2] Through the use of sensitivity analysis, an attempt has been made to identify those variables which can be manipulated in order to successfully implement planned social programs designed to bring about positive changes in an urban ghetto. The issue of technological change is examined through the incorporation of a fourth variable

1

into the simulation model, in an attempt to forecast the effect of improved accessibility upon overall performance in the study area.

From these analyses it is hoped that a number of insights will emerge concerning the impact of change on urban ghettos and the effect (or lack of effect) of transportation as it relates to these developments. Special emphasis will be placed on discerning: (1) the circular-cumulative pattern of change among the variables of education, health, and income; (2) the dynamics of system behavior over time; and (3) the strategies for system change.

Theories of Social Change

Only recently, when many public plans and programs have proven obsolete even before they could be implemented, has the significance of social change become evident to many of the urban professions. Thus, planners and related urban professionals have begun to turn their attention to the theoretical constructs of sociology and economics in search of workable models of growth and change. It may be useful, therefore, to provide a brief discussion of the existing theories of social change, and to examine some of the more pertinent models of urban growth and change so as to afford some perspective for the simulation model to be applied in the present analysis.

The Nature and Mechanisms of Social Change

One of the basic tenets of sociology is that the process of *interaction*—the interplay between the action of an individual and the actual or expected reaction of others—constitutes the core of social life and human behavior. (The simplest unit of sociological analysis—as distinct from psychological studies—consists not of solitary individuals, but of at least a pair of individuals mutually influencing each other's behavior through the process of interaction.) Social interaction may be viewed as the totality of behavior patterns of any social group, community, or society. Where conditions are relatively static, these behavior patterns gradually undergo minor modifications, but remain essentially the same through time. Forces may be introduced into the social system, however, that result in dramatic shifts in human motivation and/or may create new value orientations. These shifts also may result in changes in behavior patterns, in roles, and in the structural and functional components of the social system. Groups that cannot (or will not) adapt to meet new conditions may lose out in the struggle for social support. The fact that such groups do change, however, means that their "competitors" also must change, and changes carried out by these "rivals," in turn, stimulate other changes. Such conditions of change and counterchange, in fact, produce a dynamic society.

Thus, when sociologists speak of social change they mean structural alterations in parts or in whole social systems not the mere repetition of certain social activities or the iteration of various procedures, rewards and sanctions, or facilities and personnel within an existing social structure. Such iterations are social processes; they do not automatically lead to social change.[3]

Two basic and partially competing sets of theories in sociology endeavor to explain social change. The first set of theories studies the *nature* of social change (the magnitude, quality, kind, direction, and pace of change), endeavoring to explain it in terms of the mutual relations which exist among various subsystems and elements of society (e.g., theories dealing with conflict, malintegration, adaption, and cultural interaction). The second set attempts to determine the dominant (generally internal) factor or *mechanisms* of change, e.g., change in technology, economic and political institutions, ideology.

Difficulties arise, however, in the application of information acquired in these two theoretical spheres, since very often aspects of both approaches are interrelated. Knowledge dealing with the mechanisms of change, for the most part, has been applied in the formulation of policies for economic development or in efforts to modernize traditional and developing countries, when, for example, various economic, social, educational, or health service reforms are introduced. Without a thorough study of the nature of change, however, it is difficult to determine in the process of upgrading a static society (or groups within a society) to its full potential whether it is more important to expand the economic base first, or to initially introduce certain reforms in the social and economic organization of the society. For example, many of the economic development programs directed toward the needs of an area such as Appalachia have focused on the provision of new economic opportunities and facilities, such as improved transportation, which are seen to augment these economic potentials. Without a parallel effort to modify individual and collective attitudes of the people in such areas through certain social reforms, however, such programs may produce unanticipated consequences from the initial economic inputs. Increased skills, coupled with improved transportation facilities, have made it possible for the more productive segment of the society to leave an economically depressed region, leaving behind an even greater cycle of poverty for those who cannot, or will not, participate in the economic development programs. Efforts to regulate the processes of urbanization often can be inefficient, as experiences

from countries with centrally planned economies have shown. Only a broader
knowledge of the factors and mechanisms leading to urbanization can make this
regulation more efficient.

Factor or Mechanism Theories

Numerous attempts have been made to formulate theories concerning the
factors or mechanisms contributing to the processes of social change. In general,
these theories can be broadly grouped as: (1) *linear theories*, in which the
assumption is that social evolution proceeds only in one direction and will not
return to previous states; and (2) *cyclical theories*, concerned with historical
rhythms, repetitions, and cycles.

The "cultural-lead-and-lag" theories and various "successive-stages"
theories are examples of the linear approach to social change. Cultural-lead-and-
lag theories assume that society in general can be characterized by a close
integration, maintained in a slow-moving, dynamic equilibrium. Disturbances in
this evolving pattern of society create stresses and strains, and may result in one
phase stepping out in the lead of change, while other phases cling to traditional
forms. Successive-stages theories suggest that every society or segment of
society must develop in accordance with an evolutionary pattern, and pass
through one by one an inevitable series of growth stages.[4] For the most part,
these theories have been criticized as being simplistic and offering only partial
explanations of change phenomena in society.

A cyclical theory of social change, on the other hand, must be a very complex model if it is to describe the complicated reality of social processes. Chapin
has suggested what an adequate cyclical theory would be like.[5] He asserts that
every element of society has its own law of change, which is "probably cyclical
and may be periodic." When the cycles or periods of a number of the most
important societal elements are synchronous (i.e., are in rhythm), fluctuations in
the vigor and vitality of the society as a whole are discernible. When a majority
of societal elements are on the upward slope of their cycles, the society is "in a
state of efforescence."[6] When a majority of societal elements have passed their
peak, however, the society may pass into a state of social decay. Chapin suggests
that growth, temporary equilibrium, and disintegration is the normal cycle of
social traits, and that societal advance and decline—the result of the advance and
decline of component social institutions—is unavoidable.

Sorokin took these theories one step further by attempting to include both
cyclical and linear change in a more generalized and flexible concept of *variable
recurrence*.[7] In Sorokin's view, a society may proceed in a given direction for a

time, and thus appear to conform to a linear formula. Eventually, however, as a result of forces that are internal to the society itself (what Sorokin called "the principles of immanent change"), a shift in direction occurs and a new period of development is ushered in. The new trend may be linear or it may be oscillating, perhaps in conformance with some particular type of curve. In any case, the new trend also reaches limits and still another trend takes its place. In the course of these irregular changes, society may partially return to one of its previous states, thus completing the nearest thing to a cycle that can be expected.

Technological and Economic Factors

The most significant variables from among the numerous factors affecting social change are technological and economic in nature. Theories built around these factors assume that technological changes or changes in economic institutions underline all other changes, and even determine the direction and content of these secondary changes. Ogburn, in his well-known theory, assumed that many aspects of contemporary industrial society—its tensions, conflicts, and disorganization—could be explained in terms of cultural lags.[8] Ogburn defined the concept of cultural lag as "the strain that exists between two correlated parts of culture that change at unequal rates of speed." Thus, Ogburn asserted that in our rapidly changing society, technological change sets the pace, with the rest of culture lagging behind. Social innovations that might keep the society integrated are held back by some sort of inertia, resulting in stress on social organization following unequal rates of change. Whereas a close integration was once maintained in a slow-moving equilibrium of all parts of the society, as technology steps out in the lead of change and many social organizations cling to traditional forms, breaks appear. Conflict replaces accommodation, and unity yields to disorganization. While this sequence may seem to offer a plausible explanation of the conflict and disorganization of modern society, it fails to reveal the essence of the processes that produce these social problems, i.e., it looks at effects and presumes causes. Thus, such factor theories bear the stigma of mechanistic interpretations of social causality. They tend to disregard the fact that changes in technology do not come automatically but are dependent upon certain preconditions in the society.

As Musil points out, the interaction between technology and social organization in an urban society often is contrary to that assumed by cultural-lag theories.[9] Technological structures in urban areas (e.g., transportation, communication, and other aspects of the urban infrastructure) often lag behind more rapidly changing life styles and, as a consequence, retard social change. Moreover a lag often exists between various forms of technology. The discrepancy between the inertia of physical and technological structures in urban areas and the high variability in the needs of society is a well-known enigma that urban planners must face in rapidly changing societies. This discrepancy, however, may also serve as an important stimulus to the development of new urban technologies.

Modern Factor Theories of Social Change

The nineteenth century was dominated by attempts to develop "great theories" of social evolution and change. More contemporary efforts, however, have sought a more pragmatic theory of social change, concentrating primarily on three related problems: determination of units of change, measurement of change, and identification of the directions of change. The more elementary models of social change build on earlier linear theories by focusing on the cumulative growth at the macroscale that can be observed in some areas of technology and science, as well as the economy. Studies have shown, for example, that the average increase in productivity over an entire economy of a large industrial country may follow a fairly regular pattern, evidencing gradual increases over considerable periods of time.[10] However, recognition of the fact that many social and economic phenomena do not develop gradually or with measurable regularity, and that lags are evident at the microscale in the economic and social development of particular segments of a society (e.g., the urban ghetto and rural areas of poverty), has led to the development of other models. The simplest among these models is the "stairstep" notion of social change,[11] used primarily by historians to classify and describe stages of social and cultural evolution, e.g., by using dominant technologies at various periods of history. An example of this approach is Mumford's classification of eotechnic, paleotechnic, and meotechnic phases of human history.[12]

These elementary models of growth have been followed by various contemporary notions of *developmental cycles* that exhibit long-term upward trends. Such models adequately describe not only macrosocial changes (e.g., cycles of technological innovation), but also a wide range of microsocial phenomena of change.[13] Examples of this latter point include the sequence of innovation and its accommodation in production enterprises, the introduction of new consumer products and the subsequent stabilization of buying patterns, or the process of growth in the number of employees in large organizations. Long-term cycles with partial retrogressions are frequent characterizations of business cycles in market economies.

Various growth models have been developed on the basis of mathematical functions. The *exponential function*, for example, has been applied primarily to growth in technology and science. Exponential functions, however, can be used with equal effectiveness to model such phenomena as the growth of the world's population in the past two centuries.[14] *Logistic curves*—sometimes called autocatalytic curves—originally applied in the biology of population growth, are suited with various modifications for modeling technological growth, for forecasting long-term patterns of consumerism, and for the study of many other social phenomena as well.[15] These models have been applied in the analysis of complex changes in urban population concentrations and the demand for space in housing.

While most of these models assume cumulative long-term upward trends, other models exist in which only one subsystem of society—primarily the science-technology complex—develop cumulatively. Other subsystems, however, do not exhibit such cumulative growth trends, but rather are characterized by trendless cycles (e.g., artistic styles, ideological structures, cultural patterns, fads and fashions).

Conflict, Malintegration, Adaptation, and Interaction Theories of Change

Many social theorists have abandoned attempts to "explain" social change in broad cultural terms, and have instead turned their attention to those forces which produce change in contemporary society. Burgess, one of the early theorists to examine these issues in the urban context, applied the term "social adjustment" to refer to "the adaptation to social change by modification of social institutions," and suggested that functional relationships among individuals and institutions may be altered by changes in demographic, economic, or social processes.[16] Ogburn's theory of "cultural lag" envisioned technology changing more rapidly in urban society than other aspects of social organization—such as culture, social knowledge, and law, therefore suggesting that technological development, unless properly guided, would produce instability and disruption in the social order. The economic and technological factors in social organization are also prominent in the human ecology school, developed in the mid-twenties at the University of Chicago by Park and his associates. An important reformulation of the technological emphasis was presented by Cottrell in *Energy and*

Society (1955), in which the forms and uses of energy are related to the processes of social change.

A common denominator of this group of theories is that they seek to explain social change in terms of the inner processes of social systems. According to the *conflict theories*, for example, social change results from a sharpening of conflict between social groups within a society.[17] Implied in this set of theories is the assumption that there is little reason for change in socially integrated societies, i.e., societies with a high degree of social consensus. Conversely, a diverse, heterogeneous society, lacking social cohesiveness among its component groups, is characterized by frequent conflict and therefore, potential social change.

Similarly, the *malintegration theory* explains change in terms of incompatibilities between different parts of the social system (between different demands of the economy and the family, between the family and religious institutions, between personality and the demands made upon an individual by social institutions, and so on). Another important source of inconsistency is inherent in the nature of role expectations in modern society. The adult male must play many roles—husband, father, lover, breadwinner, boss, employee, and so forth—and these roles frequently place conflicting demands on him. The adult female is faced with similar role conflicts; she must be a mother to her children, but in the extended absences of the father, she must also be a disciplinarian, and with increasing frequency, the working wife provides an additional source of family income (a role that may come in conflict with the other demands placed upon her). A number of pertinent studies have examined the role conflicts arising as a consequence of a matriarchal family structure, in which the woman is the head of the household, particularly with reference to urban ghetto families.

A functionally oriented version of malintegration theory seeks to explain social change by emphasizing the "needs" of any segment of society for compatibility among its component parts. This *adaptation theory* of change has two variants: in order to "survive," each social system must adapt to external stimuli arising in its broader environment; and there is a continual need for mutual adaptation of various subsystems within a society (e.g., the family must adapt to the economy of an industrial society by limiting its size and becoming more mobile). According to the theory of adaptation, the greater the differentiation and complexity of a system, the more ready its adaptation to change in other external systems. For example, countries with broadly differentiated (diverse) economies are less vulnerable than those with one-sided economies (e.g., one-crop or one-industry economies). This concept is confirmed by economic and social crises occurring in urban areas with nondifferentiated

economic bases,[18] or among urban groups faced with limited economic
opportunities.

The basis of the *cultural interaction* theory of change has been succinctly
explained by Cohen as follows:

> When the members of two cultures interact there is a tendency for cul-
> tural change to occur or for an acceleration of cultural change to occur.
> The reason for this is not simply that each brings new items of culture
> to the other, but that the increase in the number of cultural items avail-
> able to each leads to the possibility of new combinations of these items.
> [19]

It would appear that this process applies when the two interacting cultures are
approximate to one another in the level of their development. When there are
wide disparities between the two cultures, however, the dominant culture will
"acculturate" the subordinate culture, leaving little opportunity for a multiplier
effect.

Processes of Social Change

Contemporary efforts to study social change also have focused on models
that attempt to simulate as accurately as possible certain process aspects of social
change. Many of these partial models could not have been formulated without the
grounding of the "classic" theories. This applies to models of industrialization
and modernization, which benefit from the paradigm of social change created by
Marx, as well as sociological models of the urbanization process built on the
foundations laid by Durkheim, Toennies, Maine, and others.

In contemporary society, a given locality is linked through a complex
communication system to the total society of which it is a part. Therefore, many
forces producing social change are generated from outside the community.[20]
For example, a national emergency, such as a war or economic depression, may
require measures over which the members of a given community have little
control. Under such circumstances they experience *regimentation*, a process
leading to decreased autonomy by local people over their own affairs. Many
communities also feel the impact of numerous features of dominant metropolitan
areas. Thus, it is possible to speak of the process of *urbanization* as covering not
only the movement of people to cities, but also the movement of urban ways
and life styles to rural areas where they are adopted by those persons still living
there.[21]

Two somewhat related processes of change are *industrialization* and *mechanization*. The process of industrialization involves mass employment; it increases the social heterogeneity as far as occupational strata are concerned; and it usually is accompanied by unionization to deal with those guiding the mass production processes in the economy. The process of mechanization, in turn, results from the introduction of new technologies whereby machines tend to replace men. Both of these processes of change have a significant impact on a given community and on the society at large.

Still another process of change is *commercialization*, whereby more aspects of life are brought under the influence of the entrepreneur. For example, recreation, which at one time was virtually free, since it took place in informal groups and involved participation by the people themselves, has become a big business, with people willing to pay considerable sums each year to enjoy activities that fill their leisure time.

A final process of change necessitating social adjustment is *secularization*, or the tendency to substitute rationality for tradition. Contemporary society offers numerous examples of this phenomenon, such as the changing role of religious institutions and the family and the rise of the educational system as a socialization mechanism.

These processes are part of the American and western European way of life, and few members of these societies can escape their impact. These processes not only characterize areas of life in which social change is occurring, but typify certain major adjustments that people of a society must make to the dynamic forces about them.

From this brief, selective survey of concepts relating to the types and directions of social change it may be seen that there are several parallel and partial theories that complement each other in dealing with changes in various parts of society. As yet, methodological difficulties involved in the development of complex analytical models have proven to be insurmountable. Therefore, sociology has been limited to partial theories of change.

Models of Urban Growth and Change

During the past decade, a series of models has been developed, primarily in the United States, that have as their objective the discovery of "fundamental laws" of growth and change in urban society. Most of these models are designed for deterministic systems, where planning is predictive and predicated on principles (assumptions) governing the behavior of basic decision-making units, e.g., households, business firms, and public bodies. These models attempt to simulate the behavior of many diverse elements that contribute to the expansion of urban areas. The results of these models, however, have not been very promising. As one recent survey of urban growth models has concluded:

> The numerous researches undertaken in the United States with considerable resources by very diverse approaches have been abandoned, except those on partial models. . . . It would seem useful to direct oneself towards partial models allowing the appreciation of consequences of decisions important for planning (transportation, zoning, etc.).[22]

Despite a lack of success evident in these first attempts to model the growth processes of the total urban system, their significance should not be underestimated. They have raised many important questions that previously have been rather vaguely defined.

Lowry's Classification of Urban Models

Lowry offers three basic categories of urban models: *descriptive, predictive,* and *general planning models.*[23] Each category varies in effectiveness, complexity, and purpose. According to Lowry, descriptive models replicate the essential features of an already observed process of urban change. Such models are of value because they reveal much about the structure of the urban environment, and in some cases, reduce the apparent complexity of the city to the more rigorous format of mathematical equations. Early models of Park and Burgess (concentric ring theory), Hoyt (sector theory), and Harris and Ullman (multinuclei theory) are examples of such descriptive models.[24] Such models frequently are concerned with the distribution of households or firms in urban areas, and may lead to the construction of so-called "iso-rent" or "iso-income" curves. Wingo, for example, hypothesized that each household, wishing to maximize its net income, seeks to locate housing as near as possible to place of work, and thereby produces "zones" based on the ability to afford a particular location.[25] This phenomenon, in turn, creates increases in the competition for land. Important descriptive models have been developed by the staff of the Rand Corporation in connection with its research on urban transportation and its relation to urban growth.[26]

Unfortunately, descriptive models do not explain the mechanisms of urban growth. Neither do they satisfy the urban planner's need for information about an uncertain future, nor assist decision-makers in choosing among alternative public programs. Descriptive models utilizing the simulation capacity of the computer are rare, and in most cases are poorly developed; their application is largely heuristic.

Predictive models are employed in forecasting the occurrence of dependent events given the occurrence of related, independent events. The most familiar of the predictive models are those based on regression analysis and simultaneous equations. Less familiar but of growing importance are models based on canonical correlation analysis and similar multivariate techniques. Both types, however, are based on the assumption that there is a causal sequence,[27] that is, that variables are functionally related and that the direction and probably magnitude of future (dependent) events can be estimated given knowledge of their causes, which usually are assumed to lie in a select number of independent variables.

Explicative models are a special type of predictive model, which attempt to explain the mechanisms of the distribution of urban activities so as to ensure an economic or even a social optimum. One of the more important of these models was developed as part of the Penn-Jersey Transportation Study.[28] The objective of this model was to predict the economic behavior of households in the choice of places of residence. It is assumed that households seek to maximize, at an equal level of satisfaction, the sum that they can devote to the land on which they will reside. To this group of models also belong the Chicago opportunity model (Hamburg and Lathrop), the land value model (Brigham), and the Pittsburgh model (Lowry).[29] Recently, attempts have been made to find social as well as economic mechanisms that determine the location of households. These studies have concentrated on explanations as to the location of certain population groups by means of the "house class" concept, and the competition of these classes for housing space.[30]

Although more practical and useful to planners than the simple deterministic models, most predictive models implicitly assume linearity and direct causal relationships—a fact that violates the interrelatedness, multicollinearity, and feedback behavior of human relationships. Since simulation models ordinarily attempt to integrate these relationships into their format, they may be viewed as a particular kind of predictive model, which is more responsive to nonlinear factors in society.

The final class of models, the *planning models*, necessarily incorporate the method of conditional prediction, but go further in that outcomes are evaluated in terms of planning goals.[31] Simulation models increasingly fall into this category, possibly in an attempt to provide more effective policy guidance to decision-makers. The essential features of planning models, according to Lowry, are: (1) the specification of alternative programs that might be chosen as an optimal approach; (2) the prediction of the consequences of choosing each alternative; (3) the scaling of these alternatives according to a common numeric standard; and (4) the determination of an optimal solution in terms of yield on invested resources (cost-benefit or cost-effectiveness analysis). Since a wide range of possible decisions is assumed in these models, and thus also variability in the possible types of urban growth, these approaches are sometimes referred to as *stochastic models*. An example of such a planning model is the *Empiric goal-programming technique*. [32] This model creates and evaluates alternative policy decisions through a linear programming algorithm set to optimize given policy objectives.

Simulation Models

Simulation models differ little from the general types of planning models in terms of method and complexity. In fact, they are included in all three categories of Lowry's classification. Should any difference exist, it would lie in perspective and purpose. The intent of these models is more to duplicate real-world conditions in a realistic and comprehensive way than to reduce reality to a mathematically rigorous but behaviorally inaccurate format, a characteristic common to the more traditional deterministic and predictive models.

As a consequence of the quantitative revolution in the behavioral and social sciences, which occurred in the late fifties and early sixties, the number and complexity of computer simulation programs have increased in recent years in proportion to advances in computer design and machine language. Most of these models have originated from the economic and engineering disciplines, presumably reflecting their mathematical orientation. Sociology, geography, and city planning have contributed somewhat fewer simulation programs.

Of the social science disciplines, economics has developed the greatest number and diversity of simulation models. Reflecting an interest in business fluctuations and growth, economic modeling has effectively encompassed single- and multisector, trade cycle, and capital growth theory. The models that capture these processes range from the very sophisticated, which use linear stochastic equations as their structure, to those that rely on single or multiple estimating equations. Less varied are the geographic scales of these models. Most tend to be concentrated at the national or global scale; very few deal with regional or local processes. Moreover, the latter largely focus on the relationships of firm and market operations, and especially those relationships between the organization of land and the pattern of land rents. Not unsurprisingly, these and the other economic models stress the interconnection of economic variables. The social variables of age, health, and education are largely ignored, although this bias has partly changed in recent years. Models developed by Forrester on urban, industrial, and world dynamics have attempted to incorporate several social variables into an econometric system.

Less well developed are the simulation models emanating from sociology. Of these, the more advanced have some form of relationship with economics. In fact, the most sophisticated deal with the behavior of national socioeconomic systems, such as those constructed by Martin Shubik for several Latin American countries.[33] Less advanced models emphasize the traditional thrust of sociological research, including path analysis, role playing, social stratification, peer influences, deviant group behavior, and group values. Their intent is to discern the workings of groups and the social institutions that guide group actions. Only rarely do they examine urban conditions, and even then the analysis is oriented toward social processes, not urban processes per se.

This absence of disciplinary concern for urban conditions is attenuated only slightly by the spatial orientation of geography. As a science that measures and evaluates areal distributions, geography has been forced to examine those urban processes having a spatial context. Simulation models have been constructed by geographers to capture these processes, and such models have been most successful at replicating the diffusion pattern of information and goods, the development and use of land, and the pattern of urban-regional growth.[34] These models have, of course, a predominant spatial orientation; therefore they provide limited insight into most urban conditions.

Seemingly, only engineering and city planning have developed coherent and reasonably advanced models of urban conditions per se. Both are prescriptive disciplines, tending to be concerned with practical measures. Clearly the most significant contribution by engineering to the development of simulation models of urban conditions has been in the field of transportation; the simulation routines of traffic flow and land use have nearly all originated from this field. Also important are the optimization models based on linear and dynamic programming techniques. Examples include *Quadatt, Empiric Programming, Topaz,* and the *Penn-Jersey model.*[35] Each has been instrumental in assessing the impacts of policy proposals and in allocating capital facilities in an optimal fashion. Urban planning has made use of these models, applying each to a variety of land-use and transportation problems. However, the main thrust of model research and construction in urban planning has focused on the evaluation of policy impacts. These models directly correspond to the planning models described by Lowry. Somewhat less emphasis has been placed on the development of the more traditional gaming and predictive models. Gaming models have been relatively simple, and very largely concerned with the analysis of political processes and land-use patterns, particularly those centering on the pattern of growth about capital facilities.

In contrast, predictive models have dealt with a variety of urban conditions, including the processes of residential change, land development, housing deterioration, and the like. Yet none have tried to duplicate the general socioeconomic processes of the urban ghetto.

Apparently, then, the traditional academic disciplines have failed to examine the workings of the urban ghetto except in a partial and mutually exclusive way. In the main, their models have tended to be of a general nature and oriented toward both disciplinary consideration and problems on a national or regional level. A major exception, however, is to be found in Forrester's groundbreaking work on urban dynamics, which serves as the point of departure for this present study.

Urban Systems Dynamics

Forrester's concept of urban dynamics is perhaps the best known (and most ambitious) of the existing urban models. His approach offers a means for investigating complex feedback relationships between industry, housing, employment, and the population subsystem. The methodology underlying this model is derived directly from Forrester's celebrated *industrial dynamics model*.[36] While the urban dynamics model has been criticized for its limited dimensionality and for its strong ties to its creator's background in industrial management, the restrictions applied are intentional. In Forrester's words, "The model should include only those processes necessary to the creation and correction of urban decay."[37]

The urban dynamics model can be operated in either an equilibrium mode or as a growth model. The equilibrium mode examines the progress of the system from a set of initial conditions to economic stagnation over a period of 250 years. The growth model takes the area from a point of equilibrium through a fifty-year period of redevelopment. Forrester also has applied his model in the study of a number of classical urban strategies, such as providing low-cost housing or job retraining programs. His findings suggest that a number of such schemes do actual harm to his model in the long run. Thus, even a fairly constrained model can be a useful tool in pointing up unexpected results that may occur as a consequence of subsystem interaction when strategies that appear to be intuitively correct are applied to complex systems.

Forrester has made a further extension of his methodology to a *world dynamics model*. This model deals with the interrelationships among population, capital investment, natural resources, pollution, and the proportion of capital devoted to agriculture.[38] The output from this model includes, along with the first four variables mentioned above, a "quality of life" index, derived from variables that focus on pollution, crowding, the availability of food, and a

material standard of living, all of which can be measured in terms of the basic
dimensions of the model. The world dynamics model leads to some startling
conclusions as to the long-range effects of continued policies that encourage
economic and population growth.

Forrester's models are cybernetic, in that they describe the behavior of
multiloop feedback systems over time. While the specific variables included in
these models may be open to question (i.e., the quality of information in feedback loops), the general methodology offers significant promise for the analysis
of alternative urban strategies. A particular advantage of this type of model is
that the simulation permits the testing of certain assumptions in a way not
possible in reality; one cannot alter at will major public policies and expenditures
in a real urban situation simply for the sake of experimentation.

Forrester's work has stimulated further development and more diverse
applications of dynamic models. Studies are being conducted at the University of
Pittsburgh, for example, on the modeling of industrial systems in developing
countries.[39] Such models might prove useful for planning purposes by
providing insights into the probable affects of changes in economic policy or in
the structure of the industrial system. Data necessary to operate this model are
described as *technological* (types of industry, supply and flow of raw materials,
degree of automation, etc.), *economic* (sales and profits, capital accumulation,
wages, etc.), and *sociological* (demographic data, family data, religious distributions, attitudinal measures, and so forth). This model also considers external
effects such as capital assistance from other countries.

The variables of this industrial model provide some idea of the interactions
among major conceptual systems that affect the industrial system under study.
There seems to be no reason why the same techniques cannot be applied to the
components of an urban system.

Kadanoff, Voss, and Booknight have developed a dynamic systems model in
which the critical factors are real-estate transactions, construction patterns, and
the use of structures.[40] Private and public sectors are handled as interactive
components through the regulatory tools of zoning, building codes, taxing
powers, and the placement of utilities, including sewer, water, and transportation.

Models such as the *horizon planning model* and the *systemic planning model*
have been developed to aid in the analysis of stochastic behavior in urban systems and, in cybernetic terms, to develop means of control and regulation. The
horizon planning model postulates certain long-range goals for urban systems.
[41] It is recognized in this model that the urban system will undergo trans-
formations as it seeks the attainment of broad goals, and, therefore, certain
subgoals are established along the system's trajectory which are related to
different states through which the system may pass. This conceptual model

differs from traditional planning approaches, which tend to project goals in terms of present trends, attitudes, and capabilities without allowing for significant changes that may occur.

The systemic planning mechanism emphasizes the feedback process in the planning operation.[42] This model underlines the need to monitor the complexities within an urban system in a manner that will lead to recognition of the interdependence and coupling of the subsystems comprising the larger urban system. As changes occur in the output of one subsystem, the reciprocal changes in the inputs to all other subsystems must be identified. Thus, the systemic model attempts to show relationships among the major subsystems of an urban area, such that any subsystem receives input from the output of other subsystems as well as from its own output. By analyzing the model, the regulatory functions of specific system components, or of components acting in concert, can be described. If the controlling aspects of the system can be identified, then, planning for the achievement of particular goals is more easily accomplished.

All of the models cited above may be termed *cybernetic,* in that they have been developed to analyze the dynamic behavior of urban phenomena under feedback regulation processes as specified by the investigators. The models vary drastically in their generality and in the richness of information incorporated in the feedback mechanisms. All of these models are abstract representations of the real world. Nevertheless, they represent a significant breakthrough in the analysis of complex urban activities, and should provide a broad platform for the further development of more refined techniques of urban analysis.

The system dynamics models may have their greatest application in adding to the conceptual understanding of urban systems rather than for specific analysis of a problem in a particular subsystem. It is conceivable that they will provide insights into relationships between the urban subsystems that heretofore have been overlooked—this seems to be Forrester's point in *Urban Dynamics.* Those components which act as regulators in the urban system seldom have been recognized in that light, and consequently, effective control has eluded the grasp of planners and administrators.

Social Change and Urban Systems Planning

In view of the rapidity of social change, serious efforts must be mounted to seek and define the functional and dysfunctional aspects of such change. This is not an abstract problem to be left to the theorists. As unsuccessful examples in urban renewal and slum clearance bear witness, this problem must be of central concern to the planning profession.

Incompatibilities, Strains, and
Unpredictable Changes

Perhaps the most valuable lesson to be learned from existing theories of
social change is that individual elements in society experience different rates of
change. The unevenness of these changes is one of the most important concepts
for the planning of urban systems. Individual elements of urban systems not only
develop at a different pace, but very often their changes affect the structure of
the city in quite opposite ways—the simultaneous existence of centripetal and
centrifugal forces is well known. These forces find expression primarily in the
conflicts between the inertness of physical structure and the dynamics of urban
life systems, in the lags in the technology of production and transportation, and
in the factors that produce the "ghetto cycle" in an affluent society. Strikingly
few studies have dealt with the aging of the urban infrastructure. Without the
classification and analysis of the processes of aging and the replacement needs—
without the "life tables" of critical elements in the urban environment—it is
impossible to decide rationally when change is economical and expedient. At the
same time, attempts by urban authorities to catch up with the exponential
growth of technology are becoming more and more hopeless. One of the greatest
enigmas of contemporary society is the persistence of poverty when "progress
is our most important product."

The paramount issues centers on the question of how to cope with these
strains, incompatibilities, and unpredictable changes in technologies and life
styles. It is unlikely that a safe and reliable defense can be found; in fact, such a
defense mechanism, if found, would likely produce a static society with all its
social, political, and psychological implications. What is possible, however, and
seems necessary, is a modified approach to planning, and a search for various
means, if only partial, to plan for change and growth.

Better Adaptability of Urban
Systems to Change

According to the theories of social change, larger and more *differentiated*
social systems are most adaptable to rapid change. Such systems may be assumed
to have differentiated economic structures, with differentiated primary,
secondary, tertiary, and even quarternary sectors. Simultaneously, such systems
are accelerators of economic growth.[43]

Greater differentiation must go hand in hand with a receptivity to *innovation*.

From studies of economics, it has been learned that the conditions of dynamic equilibrium involve a flow of innovations, introduced into the existing economic system. At the same time, however, society is capable of absorbing only a certain amount of innovation, and therefore, there can appear what might be called an *innovation overload*. The same phenomenon applies to urban systems in general; they can be overloaded with unnecessary changes. What is needed, therefore, is better knowledge of the capacities of urban systems to absorb innovation and change.

The introduction of selectivity in the processes of innovation will require new *mechanisms of integration*. One of these mechanisms must be planning. To achieve a dynamic equilibrium in urban systems, existing techniques of planning must be significantly improved and new approaches must be developed. The traditional approach, stressing the functional and aesthetic qualities of the environment, leading to the identification of activity complexes, and culminating in some ideal spatial arrangement, is no longer adequate to deal with the problems of the urban environment. Planning must involve a more rational adaptation of the physical and spatial structure of urban areas to meet the social needs of growth and change. Increased significance must be placed on the flexibility of planning and its ability to deal with expected (and unexpected) change.

Unfortunately, there are more questions than answers. What exactly is meant by "dynamic equilibrium"? How should it be defined, and what are its criteria? Is the present equilibrium between change and continuity "dynamic," and is it desirable? It is a stable equilibrium? What are the capacities of people to accommodate change? Do these capacities vary among individuals of differing socioeconomic status and among the young, middle-aged, and older individuals? Is it necessary to introduce new, intergenerational criteria to define an acceptable pace of change? As Margaret Mead has observed, as their world and that of their children become discontinuous in times of rapid change, parents are often unable to prepare their children adequately for life.

Social change can be seen from the point of view of the social system and its subsystems, on the one hand, and from the point of view of the individual on the other. Changes that may be functional from the systemic point of view are not automatically favorable for the individual. There are those who hold that large cities are the generators of change and therefore are appropriate environments for social and technological innovations. Counterarguments are offered by those who stress the high human costs of such changes and the social disparities and inequities that often result. This controversy offers evidence that the problem of social change is not merely an academic one. Through planning, a high level equilibrium must be sought, one that can maximize both the systemic and humanistic points of view.

Cities are more than physical entities; they are sociospatial systems. While planners in the past have sought measures that would lessen the natural inertness of the physical infrastructure vis-à-vis social change and growth, it is now critical that they turn their attention to more general principles regarding social change in complex urban systems and their component subsystems.

2 Theoretical Structure of the Model

The model of dynamic change described herein is based, in large part, on concepts of economic growth and stagnation developed by Gunnar Myrdal in *An American Dilemma* and *Asian Drama*.[1] The first of these books deals with conditions facing blacks in America prior to World War II, the second with the preconditions and problems of economic growth in southern Asia. Although both books are of a general cast and do not focus precisely on current economic conditions, many problems encountered by developing nations are analogous to those in large urban ghettos in the United States. Conditions of underemployment, unemployment, malnutrition, inadequate schooling, poor health, and inadequate social capital are very much the same. Similarly, the processes that create and connect these conditions are closely related to processes described by Myrdal. For these reasons, the transfer of Myrdal's concepts of circular causation, cumulative causation, and feedback structure affords an appropriate point of departure for the framework of the present model.

The Model

The model developed herein attempts to interrelate the critical variables of income, health, education, and at a later stage, transportation. The circuity and feedback structure of the model, as illustrated in figure 2-1, should be evident. Not evident, but to be discussed, are the cumulative properties of these interrelationships and the economic and social forces that tend to inhibit circularity.

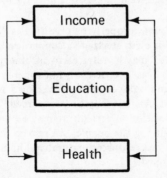

Figure 2-1. Circular-Cumulative Model

21

Model Circularity

Circular causation is based on a reciprocal interdependence of factors, namely, that a given change in one factor produces change in all other factors. This concept is the rationale underlying what Nurske and Myrdal describe as "vicious circles" in the social processes of underdeveloped countries. Nurske writes that this concept implies

> a circular constellation of forces tending to act and react upon one another in such a way as to keep a poor country in a state of poverty. Particular instances of such circular constellations are not difficult to imagine. For example, a poor man may be weak; being physically weak, his working capacity may be low which means that he is poor, which in turn means that he will not have enough to eat; and so on. A situation of this sort, relating to a country as a whole, can be summed up in the trite proposition: "a country is poor because it is poor."[2]

Inherent in the process of circular causality is an inextricable cause-and-effect relationship that operates to imprison a social or economic system in its own shortcomings; i.e., a given effect acts as a cause to a substantially similar effect. In short, the status quo tends to be perpetuated through the process of circular causation.[3]

The concept of circular causation frequently is implied in the definition of underdeveloped countries. Staley, for example, suggests that an underdeveloped country is one "characterized by mass poverty which is chronic and not the result of some temporary misfortune, and by obsolete methods of production and social organization, which means that the poverty is not entirely due to poor natural resources and hence could presumably be lessened by methods already proved in other countries."[4] Shannon cautions, however, that the term "underdeveloped" has been used carelessly and tends to be ill defined.

> An area that might more properly be classified as "developed but still impoverished," is characterized as "underdeveloped." An area that is "undeveloped" may be referred to as "underdeveloped" when the facts of the case are that it is not capable or amenable to development; it is undeveloped and impoverished and not much can be done about it. An area may be "developed," i.e., industrialization and mechanization of agriculture may have resulted in a high level of living among the people, but remain "underdeveloped" in the sense that its vast resources, natural and human, are still comparatively untapped.[5]

Exhaustive examination and appraisal of available data leads to the conclusion that more reliable indices relating to the level of living must be formulated in order to classify any area as developed or underdeveloped. Buchanan and Ellis have suggested two kinds of statistical data that are available for the purposes of measuring development: statistical indices representing the quality and texture of life as an end product; and indices that describe economic performance and explain or at least correlate with poor end-product data.[6] An example of the first type of index would be infant mortality rates; an example of the second type would be low per-capita economic productivity. Many indices applied in the present study are of a mixed type in that they relate to an end product or consequence, while also serving as measures of performance. These mixed types of indices reflect the process of circular causality.

Since in the proposed model circularity is assumed among the components of education, health, and income, movement out of a low-income ghetto is most difficult. "If any attempt is made to lift any part of this mesh of interlocking circles, there is usually a pull downward so that any sustained progress becomes almost impossible."[7] To illustrate this phenomenon, say the county board decides to use education as a lever in an attempt to break the circularity of stagnate conditions facing an urban ghetto. Assume that new schools are built, new curricula introduced, and better student-teacher ratios established. At best, these actions may result in a slight improvement in the educational level of the ghetto student. Lacking the motivation that would derive from greater opportunities and/or unable to achieve more optimal health conditions, the academic progress of the ghetto student may continue to be seriously impaired. Then too, as a consequence of predominately negative influences of the student's social and physical environment, there might not be any significant increase in educational skill, as measured on tests of achievement. In short, unidimensional solutions may produce less than optimal results, due to the phenomenon of circular causality.

Circular Cumulative Causation in the Model

The theory of circular cumulative causation assumes that change in one condition results in (causes) change in one or more other conditions *in the same direction*. Further, it is assumed that such change is independent and additive, with the effects of one factor contributing to an improvement (or diminution) in the other(s). Thus, an initial change is viewed as supported by consequential impulses, which in turn gives rise to repercussions (negative or positive) which magnify the initial change.[8] The concept of circular cumulative causation has an important parallel in the cybernetic notion of positive feedback, whereby a deviation is amplified and this amplification leads to further deviation from the initial point of measurement.[9] The process of cumulative causation provides a theoretical alternative to the argument of stagnation posited by the circularity concept.

It is hypothesized that health, education, and income are related to one another in this cumulative fashion. Accordingly, it is believed that additional units of income will contribute to additional increments of health and education, with the latter furthering an increase in income. It is also believed that this circular relationship can be broken at any point—either at income, health, or education. A given investment in health will produce a corresponding increase in education and income, which together generate a rise in health levels. Similarly, a like investment in education will produce an increase in health and income, each of which reciprocally influences academic performance. It is not hypothesized, however, that equal units of health, education, and income generate proportional levels of cumulative advance. In fact, certain of the variables—alone and in combination—are more influential than others.

The latter process is termed by Myrdal an "upward cumulative spiral," and is common to growth processes in more advanced (developed) nations. This circular cumulative process, however, need not always exist. For example, should an initial change in one condition give rise to secondary changes which tend to move in the opposite direction, the cumulative process may be seriously hampered, the system may be restored to an original equilibrium, or it may be forced to move further down an inward spiral.[10] To use a common example— and one pertinent to the present model—consider the effect of heightened discrimination in employment. Should such discrimination occur, it can be expected that rising unemployment will seriously hamper the attainment of improved health and education. Moreover, continued unemployment will eventually produce a cumulative downward movement of education, health, and income. It is important to understand this condition, for it emphasizes the concomitant impacts of certain actions and the importance of dealing with the interrelationships as a whole over a sustained period.

Feedback Loops

The dynamic behavior of systems is generated within feedback loops. According to Forrester, feedback loops are the fundamental building blocks of systems, and can be used to control the flow of information or material at

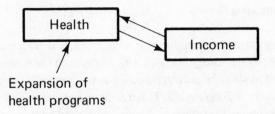

Figure 2-2. Positive Feedback

decision points within a system. Flows are accumulated to generate "system levels," an expression of system behavior.[11]

Although both positive and negative feedback loops exist in any system, the positive loops tend to be predominant in the model structure interconnecting the level variables of income, health, and education. These variables tend to generate growth processes whereby action produces results that generate still further action.[a] Under their influence, the level to which the state of the system has already risen determines the rate of further increase. Thus, the higher the system level, the faster the rate of increase in critical variables—unless, of course, some event or events intervene to alter the parameter values in the loop equation.[12] The simplest form of loop structure is illustrated in figure 2-2.

This feedback structure is vital to the movement from a low equilibrium condition, characterized by the maintenance of the status quo, to the process of upward circular cumulative causation. Circular causation will give rise to a cumulative movement only when, by interaction of all conditions in the system, a change in one of the conditions will ultimately be followed by a feedback of secondary impulses to produce a further change of that particular condition of sufficient magnitude not only to sustain the primary action, but to push it further. According to Myrdal:

> Mere mutual causation is not enough to create this process; other-
> wise the ubiquity of mutual causation would be inconsistent with
> the widely observed stability of social systems. . . . The relationship
> between the size of the coefficients of response and the speed of
> the response [will] determine whether the mutual causation results
> in stable, neutral, or unstable (up and down) conditions.[13]

---

[a] A negative feedback loop, on the other hand, seeks a goal and responds as a consequence of failing to achieve the goal; i.e., deviations are dampened through a series of approximations as the system "zeros in" on the goal.

Factors Impeding Growth

Although positive feedback loops, if unimpeded, will cause exponential growth, such growth normally interacts with elements in the surrounding system to interrupt and modify the growth process. Growth toward an upper limit is illustrated by curve A in figure 2-3. The growth process resulting from the cumulative interaction of income, health, and education approximates a some-what flatter curve, however, reflecting a smaller coefficient and a relatively slower speed of response in the cumulative growth cycle. This relationship is depicted by curve B in figure 2-3. Also important in retarding growth are the linked processes of what Myrdal terms: (1) independent counteracting changes; (2) counteracting changes released by development; and, less ambiguously, (3) time and inertia. Each of these growth-retarding factors has an additive impact, and together, they effectively inhibit the growth process. Each plays an important role in the present model, as demonstrated below.

Attitudes and Institutions

One of the most significant resistances to change in any socioeconomic system stems from the behavior patterns generated by attitudes and institutions. The rigidities of discriminatory social stratification that support racial attitudes tend to be sustained long after conditions facing minority groups may evidence

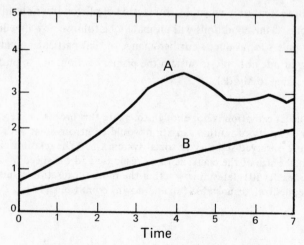

Figure 2-3. Dynamic Behavior of Systems

measurable improvement. Until these discriminatory attitudes are worn down, however, it can be expected that the response to induced change—and the speed of that response—will be slow. Institutions are part of a cultural milieu, and are not easily or rapidly moved in either direction or magnitude. Considerable time and effort is necessary for people to acquire the discipline and habits of co-operation, to want to improve their lot, and to take risks and accept change. The model employed in the present analysis reflects these conditions through relatively large delay functions in strategic variables.

The term *stereotype* was introduced to the field of social psychology by Walter Lippmann in *Public Opinion* (1922). In its literal meaning a stereotype is a metal plate, cast from a mold or a surface of type. The term was used initially by psychiatrists in a metaphorical sense to describe a frequent and almost mechanical repetition of the same gesture, posture, or word in such mental disorders as schizophrenia. Lippmann used it, however, in the broad sense of a determining tendency or a composite of ideas and attitudes which make up the "pictures in our heads." An earlier psychology called this phenomenon the "appreceptive mass."

Although it is unwise to use the term to refer to the entire internalized content of individuals, there is a definite relationship between stereotypes and the attitudes which developed or the meanings given to particular situations. A stereotype may be defined as a false, classificatory concept to which some strong emotional feeling of like or dislike, approval or disapproval, is attached.[14] Ideas and attitudes are closely tied together in the many illogical, but emotion-ally powerful and socially significant stereotypes. The stereotype, like the sound idea, has a cognitive core, carried chiefly in words or visual images, from which attitudes or overt actions may originate. Stereotypes influence social perception; moreover, they show stability and persistence. In short, the function of a stereotype is to give meaning to a situation, that is, to delimit behavior with reference to it. A stereotype defines the situation in terms of acts, potential or actual.[15] As a consequence, stereotypes—whether applied by the majority to a minority or developed within a minority in reference to those in the majority or to themselves—tend to impede change through the emergence and maintenance of expectations and acceptance. While the stereotypes held by "Archie Bunker types" (itself a stereotype) are commonly recognized, many stereotypes are, in a sense, self-imposed. Thus, the ghetto youth may lack the motivation to seek opportunities afforded him by improved education, instead following the lead of his street-corner peers (thus reinforcing stereotypes held by others). Habits of dress and speech adopted to set off one group from others may tend to feed the attitudes that give rise to and solidify stereotypes.

Counteracting Changes

On the whole, the basic assumption of unidirectional relationships within the model is realistic. Indeed, the circular cumulative process seems to provide a key to growth and development—or the lack thereof—in a stagnant, low-equilibrium social system. Nevertheless, there are exceptions to this rule, as when secondary changes move the system in a direction opposite to that of induced change. These exceptions are what Myrdal has labeled "counteracting changes."[16]

An example of a strong counteracting change may be derived from an analysis of the effects of increased education. The results of the empirical analysis that follows suggest that an increase in income ordinarily accompanies education past the twelfth grade. In the main, this relationship is sound; however, should the rate of growth in education be too rapid, as when—to take a hypothetical case—all ghetto youth obtain a college education, it can be expected that the overabundance of skilled workers will cause a sharp decline in the wages of professionals. Widespread unemployment might even result. Whatever the result, it may be assumed that the economic system will ultimately return to a state of equilibrium in response to the forces of supply and demand. Ghetto residents may be expected to continue to earn wages below those of comparably skilled workers in higher social strata. Similar situations are repeated in other equations of the model, although these tend to be more realistic of the effects produced by counteractive change.

Effects of Inertia and Time

In sharp contrast to the cumulative principle incorporated in the present model are not only the common experiences of low-level equilibria in ghetto areas and serious obstacles to development policies, but more generally the astonishing stability of most community socioeconomic systems. "Balance, far from being the fortuitous result of an unusual and obviously unstable combination of forces, seems to be the rule, not the exception."[17] The writings of political science, sociology, and anthropology all indicate that the traditionalism of culture—and its behavioral expressions—work to inhibit intended change to the extent that such change differs appreciably from the values of the affected group.[18]

Time is a critical element in maintaining and perpetuating such equilibria. When one condition changes, the reactions of other related conditions seldom are simultaneous but usually are delayed, often for considerable periods. An example of this is the relationship among levels of nutrition, the physiology and psychology of workers, and their labor output and efficiency. A rise in nutritional levels should have some short-term beneficial effects on workers' health and willingness and ability to work, and thus on productivity and income. The major effects, however, may not be realized until a new generation of workers, who have enjoyed improved nutrition from childhood, enters the labor force. Indeed, sometimes there is no reaction to some of the conditions, as when the rise in nutritional levels is only temporary. As with inertia, these happenings are introduced as delay functions in certain relationships modeled in the present analysis.

Summary

The model described herein assumes a circular relationship among the variables of education, health, and income and a cumulative advance in their system levels as a consequence of the action of positive feedback loops. These loops, in turn, are assumed to be impeded by certain effects emanating from the broader environment of the system and from certain internal growth processes. Although there is ample theoretical evidence for this form of model structure, these relationships are nonetheless assumptions and therefore, are subject to verification in the later evaluation of model projections. Hence, the confirmation of the interrelationships—and the theories on which they are based—is an important second purpose of this analysis.

3

The Study Area and Model Equations

The purpose of this chapter is to provide more discrete form to the model developed conceptually in the previous chapter. A brief description of the study area for which the model equations were developed provides a preface to this discussion. The broad characteristics of the study area should be borne in mind in examining the equations in more detail. The equations are introduced to reflect as accurately as possible the apparent workings of the education, health, and income components of the model; the transportation component is discussed in chapter 4.

The Study Area

The study area selected for the testing of the model equations coincides with the boundaries of the Miami-Dade County Model City area. It is a relatively low-income, predominantly black neighborhood in northwestern Miami, occupying an area of approximately five square miles and bounded by major expressways running east-west and north-south. During the summer of 1968, this area, like many of its northern counterparts, underwent racial unrest and riots. Indicators of social disorganization in the study area include unusually high population densities in some parts of the area, a high number of female heads of households, a large number of divorcées and unwed mothers, and a high crime and delinquency rate. In a report entitled *Germ City*, the Dr. Martin Luther King Boulevard Development Corporation[a] found that 99 percent of the property in a five-block neighborhood of the study area was owned by non-residents of the area. In many respects, characteristics of education, health, and income in the study area parallel those of many northern urban ghettos.

---

[a]The Dr. Martin Luther King Boulevard Development Corporation is a non-profit organization funded, in part, by the Model City program. The Development Corporation has stated as its objectives the implementation of six phases of inner-city development: transportation, education, commercial development, expansion of industrial-manufacturing activities, health, and housing. The Development Corporation interacts with community groups and private and public agencies in its attempts to set the stage for the implementation of Model City programs.

Education

Although the Miami-Dade County Model City area seemingly is served by an adequate number of educational facilities (there are twenty schools in the five-square-mile area), the level of educational achievement of Model City children is substantially lower than the achievement of school children in the rest of Dade County, a predominantly white, middle-class section of the Miami region. Model City twelfth-graders at Miami Northwestern, for example, scored 5.3 years behind their counterparts at Miami Coral Park in reading and 9.0 years behind the Coral Park seniors in mathematics. Similarly, the percentage of Model City children dropping out before high school graduation is significantly higher; the dropout rate of 28.6 percent is nearly eleven percentage points above the rest of Dade County. These deficiencies are translated into an adult population lacking suitable education for many types of employment. Forty-one percent of Model City residents between eighteen and twenty-one years of age have not completed high school; 38 percent between the ages of twenty-two and thirty have not graduated from high school.[1]

Health

Some progress has been made in the past twelve years toward increasing the number of available clinics and physicians in the Model City area and in reducing conditions, such as deteriorating housing, that are a detriment to good health. Nevertheless, the morbidity rates in the Model City area are still markedly higher than those in the remainder of Dade County. These levels are reflected in statistics from the health section of the "Dade County Model City Program." Specifically, although residents of the Model City area make up only 6 percent of the total county population, 25 percent of the clinic services provided by Jackson Memorial Hospital, used by the county's indigent population, are to Model City residents. The death rate (0–64) in the nonwhite population in Dade County is twice that for whites; the population in the study area is 95 percent nonwhite. Finally, the death rate among infants, perhaps one of the most significant measures of health conditions, is sixty-one deaths per thousand in the Model City area, as compared to only twenty-two per thousand in the remainder of Dade County.[2]

Income and Employment

The economy of the Miami area is based heavily on tourism and is quite susceptible to changes in national trends. National economic conditions are magnified in the region, especially within the Model City area. Income levels and their principal determinant, employment, are both extremely low in the study area. Each is strongly suggestive of the differential impact of discrimination in the Miami labor market. To illustrate this point, the mean income of Model City residents in 1970 was only $4246, as compared to $8827 for the Miami area as a whole. Employment statistics are similarly skewed: approximately 36 percent of heads of households in the Model City area in 1970 were unemployed, whereas the overall unemployment rate in the Miami-Dade County area was only 4 percent. More important, of those Model City residents employed, most have jobs in relatively low-paying blue-collar (44 percent) and service (36 percent) positions. Only 19 percent of the Model City labor force works in white-collar positions.[3]

Transportation

Residents of the study area are relatively dependent upon public transit, there being an average of 0.80 automobiles per household in the Model City area as compared with 1.12 per household for the rest of Dade County. Transit service in terms of area coverage and frequency has been described officially as "adequate."

The service is downtown-oriented and therefore somewhat deficient in serving other destinations of Model City's residents. In comparison with the automobile, one-bus rides take as much as three times the time required to reach the same place by auto. If an additional bus ride involving a transfer is included, the ratio of bus to auto travel time increases four-to-one. Two major travel attractions for Model City residents—downtown and Miami Beach—require 45-minute bus rides from the community. Other areas accessible only by a two-vehicle ride frequently require travel times in excess of an hour. In terms of employment accessibility, a 20-minute auto trip brings Model City's residents within reach of eighty percent of the jobs in Dade County; the same travel time by bus permits access to five percent of the county's employment opportunities.[4]

In short, the study area can be described as a low-income, black urban ghetto. At best, transportation seems to be marginally adequate in terms of serving the basic social and economic needs of the area. Its education, health, and income levels are typical of comparable areas in the urbanized Northeast and along the West Coast. Other social and demographic conditions in the study area are similarly deficient, serving to exacerbate the low education, health, and income levels of the ghetto. Their effect is to trap the study area in the kind of circular, downward, cumulative spiral described in the previous chapter.

Model Equations

The equations described in this chapter are further amplified in the computer printout contained in appendix A. The letters L, R, and A to the right of each equation in appendixes A and B refer to the type of equation, whereas the figures (e.g., 1-7) identify the location of the equation in the model. There are three kinds of equations used in the DYNAMO programming language. L refers to a level equation; this equation expresses the behavior of some component in the model over time. R identifies a rate equation; these are used to regulate the flow of material or information to and from a level equation. According to Forrester, rate equations are the statements of system policy. They determine how the available information is converted into an action stream."[5] They are, in short, the strategic variables or "decision points" of a system. "A" denotes an auxiliary equation. Auxiliary equations are the building blocks of a dynamic system model; they are used to estimate and project the essential characteristics of model behavior to a horizon year. They are always related to rate equations and, in the model developed here, are linked to the rate equations in a hierarchical manner. Appendix B provides a further definition of the auxiliary equations applied in the model. Examination of appendix A will reveal that the model is divided into three sections or submodels: education, health, and income. Although each submodel is relatively self-contained, the organization of each, in general, is similar. A series of linked equations are allowed to vary to provide estimates of behavior of a model component (e.g., education). Since these equations are expressed as mathematical functions, component behavior is arrived at by simply adding the various equations. This behavior is expressed in terms of a "level" variable. According to Forrester, a level variable provides an index of system performance. In the present model, level variables are used to transfer information from one model component to another. As a consequence, the circularity of factors necessary to examine cumulative growth effects is satisfied.

Equations in the Submodels

The format of each major, or linked, equation in the three submodels is identical. A coefficient is used to show the contribution of a particular variable

to an index of the system, as discussed above. An example of such an index is
the dropout rate in the educational component. This coefficient is presented in
terms of a function that expresses the exact nature of the contribution to the
index variable under conditions that are known to exist in the study area. (The
value of the coefficient is determined through multiple regression analysis.)
Typically these functions are portrayed as programming statements that duplicate
the relationship between two variables. Accordingly, as the function changes in
value, so will the contribution of the equation to the index variable, and the
index variable changes correspondingly.

An example will perhaps help to clarify this process. Equation 1-7 expresses the relationship between the student-teacher ratio and the dropout rate
in the study area. The coefficient assigned to this equation is 0.10. The magnitude of the dropout rate is expressed through the notation DROPTS. As DROPTS
varies from 28.98 to 28.70, the contribution of the function "student-teacher
ratio" changes from 0.28899 to 0.28871. Thus it may be concluded that a
change in the student-teacher ratio will only slightly affect the dropout rate.
Adding together the several linked equations in each submodel (seven in the case
of education) results in an estimate of the overall performance of that major
component in the total model.

Hierarchical Linkages and Feedback Loops

In the analysis that follows, the value of the function in these equations is
introduced by one of two means: through hierarchically linked equations that
approximate the condition of the function over time, or through feedback loops
from related equations in different submodels. In the first approach, the function
tends to increase arithmetically; in contrast, a geometric change in interrelationships between variables described by the function may result from the
second approach. This latter change is a consequence of the near exponential
growth generated by feedback loops. Equation 1-7 is illustrative of the hierarchical type, whereas equation 1-36 is typical of the feedback approach. When
combined, these processes generate the dynamics of systems behavior.

It is important to emphasize the significance of the three index variables.
They are intended to express general conditions of the study area over the period
1960-70. In a subsequent chapter, a sensitivity analysis will be conducted on
these key variables. Since changes in these variables are produced by changes in
the equations that estimate system behavior, the general conditions of the model—
and the conclusions to be drawn from this analysis—are predicated on the accuracy
of each index in representing the actual behavior of the system over time.

The Education Submodel

The assumed interaction in the education component is illustrated in figure 3-1. Of the many factors that may affect academic achievement, eight were identified through regression analysis as particularly significant (see table 3-1). Five of these factors—student-teacher (teacher aide) ratio, teacher quality, school facilities, and health—were found to be nominally important. Of greater importance were student body quality, student economic background, and student family background. Each of these factors contributed significantly to the total variance of academic achievement, as measured by performance scores,[6] and, less directly, as measured by dropout rates (the principal surrogate for academic achievement in the present study) and attendance statistics. A constant was included in the model to accumulate the unexplained variance.

Student-Teacher Ratio

A small but positive contribution to academic performance appears to derive from a low student-teacher ratio. This finding is at variance with the con-

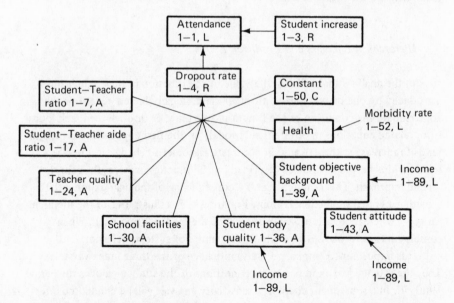

Figure 3-1. The Educational Component of the System Model. *Note:* An incoming arrow to a variable indicates an input of data from another model. Those without an arrow imply that data is supplied internally through the interaction of positive and negative feedback loops.

Table 3-1
Relationships in the Education Submodel

Dropout Rate from: Independent Variable	Coefficient	Equation
Teacher-student ratio	0.010	1-7
Teacher aide-student ratio	0.015	1-17
Teacher quality	0.019	1-24
Number of school facilities	0.017	1-30
Student body quality	0.080	1-36
Student background	0.157	1-39
Student attitudes	0.171	1-43
Health level	0.050	1-46

clusions of the Coleman Report, which suggests "a consistent lack of relationship to achievement among all groups under all conditions to adjustments in the (student-teacher) ratio",[7] and the writings of Kohl, Clark, Kozol, and Herdon, which suggest that "smaller classes and better counseling [do] not constitute sufficient solutions to the failure of schools."[8] The relationship does find support in the writings of other educational theorists, for example, articles by Edward [9] and Keliher,[10] which report a significant contribution by the teacher to student achievement. These articles also report evidence of a strong relationship between the emotional development of the child and the frequency of communication with the instructor. Edward maintains that "inharmonious classroom relationships (resulting from overcrowding) mitigate against the development of social skills necessary to good personal and social adjustment." [11] Keliher and Cannon, in turn, relate the effectiveness of such skills to academic performance.[12] Hence, despite contradictory evidence in the literature, there seems to be some validity in the assumed contribution of a low student-teacher ratio to academic achievement as expressed in equation 1-7.

The exact nature of the relationship between the student-teacher ratio and the dropout rate is given in figure 3-2. The relationship is only slightly positive. Change in the ratio will affect only slight modifications in the dropout rate. This conforms to the logic advanced by several prominent educators, notably Kohl and Clark,[13] and suggests the futility of making adjustments in this ratio to improve academic achievement. Change in the ratio itself is introduced in the model through a series of equations relating increases in the student population to like increases in the number of teachers.

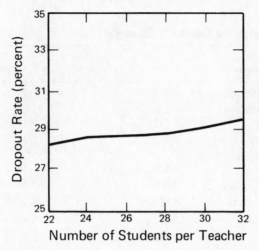

Figure 3–2. The Dropout Rate as a Function of the Student-Teacher Ratio

Teacher-Aide-Student Ratio

Associated with the student-teacher ratio is the effectiveness of nonteaching paraprofessionals—teacher aides, VISTA volunteers, and Teacher Corps members —in the improvement of academic achievement. Several descriptive studies, including those by Richardson (1969), Bahr (1969), and Weed (1970), as summarized in a 1971 article by Taylor,[14] report an improvement in student grades following the introduction of these personnel. Thus, Taylor concludes that "projects of this type tend to improve the communication process between student and teachers with respect to subject matter context,"[15] by relieving the teachers of routine classroom duties that demand time away from this communication process. Statistical studies report mixed results: Freund (1965) showed that children improved significantly in attitude and skills, while there was no significant academic improvement as measured by achievement test scores; whereas a study by Taylor (1970), using chi-square tests as criteria, revealed "a significant impact upon student performance in the positive direction."[16] Thus, there is some evidence to suggest a measurable impact by teacher aides upon the academic work of students, and particularly upon their emotional health.

The submodel (equation 1–17) suggests a positive (0.015) relationship between the use of teacher aides and academic performance. As shown in figure 3–3, this relationship is curvilinear; the effectiveness of teacher aides tends to first increase with class size and then decrease, being most significant with groups of

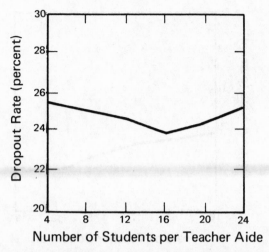

Figure 3-3. The Dropout Rate as a Function of the Student-Teacher-Aide Ratio

fifteen to twenty students. Edward maintains that groups of fifteen to eighteen are the optimal size for work with disadvantaged children.[17] Needless to say, this relationship only exists if the aides are well prepared and are understanding of the needs of children.

Change in this ratio was introduced in the same fashion as in the case of the student-teacher ratio, that is, through a series of rate and level equations that modify the value of the projected dropout rate resulting from increased use of teacher aides. Change is projected to be .05 percent per year. A base of two (teacher aides) is given; hence, the value of the ratio changes fairly rapidly, affecting the contribution of equation to the dropout rate in like fashion.

Quality of Teaching Staff

According to the Coleman report, the characteristics of teachers (education, verbal ability, salary) are second only to the characteristics of the student in their impact upon academic achievement. Perhaps more important, the quality of teaching seems to have a greater impact upon black children than upon any other group. Using this factor alone in a regression analysis, Coleman's analysis found that it explained some 9.53 percent of the total variance in academic achievement by black children, but only 1.82 percent for whites. This relationship corresponds roughly to the generally greater sensitivity of the minority student to his or her social environment.[18] The implication is that the effect

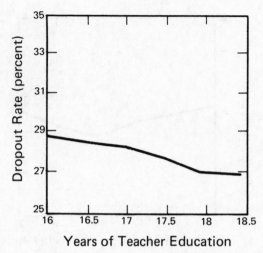

Figure 3-4. The Dropout Rate as a Function of Teacher Quality

of good teachers is greatest upon minority group children, and that a given investment in upgrading teacher quality will have the most effect on achievement in underprivileged areas.[19]

Equation 1-24 in the present model expresses this relationship. Quarter-years of education past the college degree are used to reflect the quality of teaching personnel, expressed by the varying magnitude of dropout rate as related to teacher quality. Use of this index is supported by Coleman, who found a strong (positive) correlation between student academic achievement and the academic preparation of teachers.[20]

The exact relationship between teacher quality and academic performance is shown in figure 3-4. A curvilinear association exists, with the effects of teacher quality increasing with years of advanced education. The model postulates a base of sixteen years' education, with annual increases of 0.05 in schooling. As change in the ratio proceeds, this value is entered into the sub-model, causing the degree of contribution to academic achievement to rise.

School Facilities

A general relationship exists between educational achievement and the resources available to the student. Nonetheless, this relationship is slight; at the national level school facilities account for only 4.24 percent of the variance explained on achievement tests, and only 5.66 percent in the South.[21] Equation 1-30 reflects this generally small relationship. The rate of building

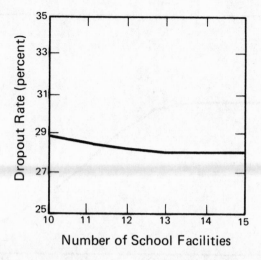

Figure 3-5. The Dropout Rate as a Function of the Number of School Facilities

construction is used as the measure of contribution by school facilities to academic performance.

Figure 3-5 depicts this relationship as curvilinear, with initial increases in the number of school facilities generating the greatest advances in academic performance. The model assumes a base of ten facilities for the study area and an annual increase of 0.05 in school facilities. Advances in this relationship are entered in equation 1-30, altering its contribution to the dropout rate.

Student Body Characteristics

One of the principal conclusions of *Equality of Educational Opportunity* (the Coleman Report) concerns the effect of other children upon a student's academic achievement. Coleman found that "attributes of other students account for far more variation in the achievement of minority group children than do any attributes of school facilities and slightly more than do attributes of staff." [22] Apparently, as the educational aspirations and backgrounds of fellow students increase, the achievement of minority group children does likewise.

The higher achievement of minority group children in schools with a greater proportion of white students is largely, perhaps wholly, related to the effects associated with the student body's education background and aspirations. These effects come not from racial composition per se, but from the better educational background and higher educational aspirations that, on the average, are found

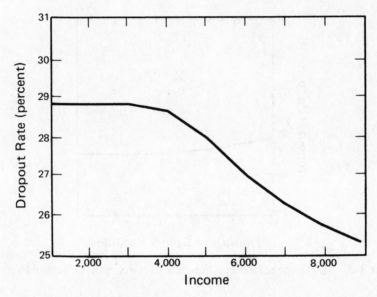

Figure 3–6. The Dropout Rate as a Function of Student Body Quality

among white students. The effects of the student body environment upon academic student achievement appears to lie in the educational proficiency possessed by that student body, whatever its ethnic or racial composition.[23]

Equation 1–36 relates these findings to the income levels of the study area. Income is used here as a rough surrogate for educational aspirations and backgrounds of the student body, since both mirror the occupations and education of parents. The exact form of the relationship is given in figure 3–6. The effect of income is basically linear, with educational performance increasing with rising income. A deviation from this relationship occurs at the $4000 level. At that level and below, income has absolutely no impact upon academic performance. Harrison attributes this to the sense of frustration and bitterness associated with low-income jobs, which the parents apparently translate into a feeling of futility with the educational process that is assimilated by their children.[24]

Change in the relationship between student body characteristics and the dropout rate is introduced in a different manner than was the case in the previous four equations. Instead of being entered indirectly through a series of hierarchically related rate and level equations, it is induced directly from the level variable, equation 1–89, of the income submodel. This is an example of a positive feedback loop, the first introduced so far. Its effect is to increase exponentially the value of student body quality in equation 1–36.

Background of Students

Equation 1-39 relates academic performance to the economic and emotional background of the student. It is hypothesized that this relationship is vitally important, accounting for nearly 16 percent of the total variance in academic performance—and that it is second only to student attitude in the contribution to this performance. As with the previous equation, income is used as a surrogate for the economic and subjective background of the student. The value of student background as related to dropout rate is entered directly from the income sub-model. The character of this relationship is assumed to be identical to that depicted in figure 3-6.

The subjective component of the equation is especially important during the high school years. Almost without exception, black parents have an exceedingly high interest in their children's education, and nearly all believe that their children should have a better occupational opportunity than they. This interest, however, is not always translated into practices that support the child's achievement. As a result, the child does not develop behavioral patterns to success academically, and a kind of emotional reaction sets in that negatively affects the child's attitude toward himself and his social environment.[25] The high coefficient in equation 1-39 underscores the surprisingly high interest by ghetto parents in their children's development and, correspondingly, the parent's inability to translate this interest into effective learning patterns.

Attitudes of Students

Recent research indicates the existence of a high self-concept as well as a high interest in school and learning among blacks. Blacks, however, seem to have a much lower sense of control over their environment than do whites,[26] and it is this lack of control that seems to undercut the academic advancement of the ghetto youth. Lacking such control (or perceiving a lack of control), the black student frequently interprets the environment as capricious and hostile. Responses are consistently in the affirmative to survey questions such as: "Good luck is more important than hard work for success," or "People like us don't have much of a chance to be successful in life." As a result of this orientation, Coleman suggests that "the virtues of hard work, of diligence and effort toward achievement appear to a child. . . as unrewarding. . . . The child is more likely to adjust to his environment, finding satisfaction in passive pursuits."[27]

Since research has established that a sense of control over one's environment has the strongest relationship to achievement, and that minority children who exhibit a sense of environmental control produce considerably higher achievement scores than those who do not,[28] equation 1-43, relating student attitudes and dropout rate, has the greatest single impact of the various equations in the education submodel. This equation also has important feedback ties to income, as expressed by the availability of good jobs. As Zito and Bardon report in their analysis of student motivation,[29] the possibility of future employment provides an important impetus to hard work and learning discipline during the high school years. Figure 3-6 approximates the effect of income upon student attitudes.

Health and Education

It is Myrdal's contention that improved health can play only a minimal role in economic growth and educational development in industrial countries, since the level of health is already quite high (relative to underdeveloped nations).[30] Research by Albert *et al.* supports the contention that improved health conditions will have relatively little impact on academic performance.[31] These findings stand in contradiction to a common assumption that diminished school attendance is a result of poor health and can be directly related to poor academic performance in ghetto schools. Albert and his colleagues, in a study of illness and health care practices among low-income children, found that very few symptoms of illness actually result in a physician being called or the individual being taken to a clinic. Nor are children kept home from school with such illnesses. Accordingly, it may be that a substantial increase in the quality and quantity of health care programs would have only a negligible impact upon the dropout rate of ghetto children. This conclusion is supported, in part, by equation 1-46, which relates the effects of morbidity upon education. The precise form of the relationship is shown in figure 3-7. The curivilinear function generated by the analysis of data in the present study underlines the significant advances in health that would be required to measurably decrease the dropout rate, thus supporting the contention that improvements in health will have only minimal effect on educational development in an already industrialized society.

The Health Submodel

The findings cited above regarding the relationship of health and the dropout rate of ghetto youths does not diminish the need to examine the impact of levels of health in terms of their impact on the dynamics of change in an urban ghetto. To the contrary, a review of the literature, complemented by the

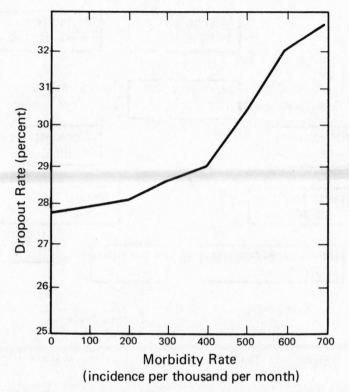

Figure 3-7. The Dropout Rate as a Function of the Morbidity Rate

Table 3-2
Relationships in the Health Submodel

Morbidity Rate from: Independent Variable	Coefficient	Equation
Physician-patient ratio	0.100	1-56
Number of facilities	0.300	1-68
Housing conditions	0.070	1-75
Education	0.123	1-81
Income	0.200	1-84

correlation and stepwise regression analyses of the present study, seems to indicate a fairly direct and significant relationship between the health levels of a ghetto area and five factors (see table 3-2), including the physician-patient ratio, the availability of health facilities, the amount of deteriorated housing, and, to complete the circular relationship among the submodels, the level of education

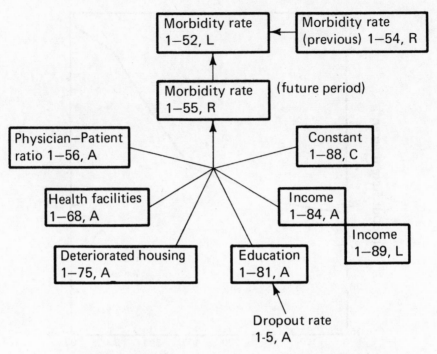

Figure 3-8. The Health Component of the System Model

and income. The interrelationship of these variables is depicted in figure 3-8. The contribution of each to morbidity rates, a surrogate for health levels, is given by a coefficient identified through multiple regression analysis. As in the education submodel, variance not explained by the five factors is accumulated by a constant.

Physician Ratio

According to studies by Robinson, Salisbury, and Lashof,[32] the level of ghetto health is measurably affected by the number and availability of physicians. Significantly, this supply is inordinately low in urban ghetto areas. In response to the migration of the white middle class, many physicians have abandoned their central-city office locations and have moved to the more affluent suburbs. In his study of Chicago, Lashof found that there were 1.26 physicians per thousand people in nonpoverty areas but only 0.62 per thousand in poverty areas. The effect of this migration has been to reduce the quality of health care in the

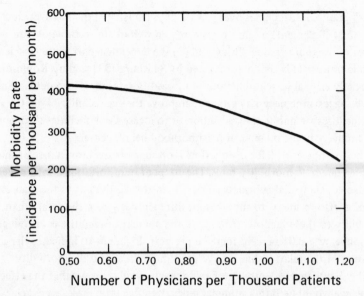

Figure 3–9. The Morbidity Rate as a Function of the Physician-Patient Ratio

ghetto and to shift significant additional burdens upon already strained urban health facilities.

Ratios similar to those found by Lashof were calculated for the Miami study area; the physician ratio in the study area is 0.76 per thousand. Equation 1–56 relates these findings, in turn, to the morbidity rate. The exact character of this relationship is presented in figure 3–9. The declining curvilinear relationship postulated in this analysis would suggest that there is relatively little impact of physician availability on health levels below a 0.80 ratio. Change in this ratio is derived from rate and level equations which relate population growth to the physician growth rate. This value is entered through the projected health from physician-patient ratio (HPHRTP), causing the contribution of the physician ratio to the morbidity rate to vary.

Health Facilities

The level of health in the ghetto, of course, is very much dependent upon the number and availability of health facilities. This relationship is particularly critical in ghetto areas because of: (1) the tendency by ghetto residents to "prefer" public health clinics over private physicians;[b] (2) the relatively high proportion (30 percent) of ghetto residents on welfare, most of whom are required to use municipal facilities; and (3) the dependence of ghetto residents on public transit. This last factor is cited by Salisburg [33] and by Robinson [34] as especially critical to the reduction of morbidity rates in urban ghettos. Such research suggests the necessity either to improve the accessibility of ghetto health facilities via public transportation or to locate these facilities throughout the community in the manner of neighborhood health centers.

The coefficient of 0.30 in equation 1-68 suggests the importance of this proximity factor to morbidity rates. The effect of transportation is introduced through a constant that subtracts a given quantity—equivalent to the inaccessibility of ghetto residents to suburban health facilities—from the total urban accessibility to these facilities. Change in the number of facilities is introduced in the model as a 0.01 percent increase per year. Figure 3-10 indicates the general nature of the relationship between health facilities and the morbidity rate. The slight (inverse) curvilinear relationship would suggest that the effects of such change would be rather minimal unless significant increases were achieved in the number of facilities, i.e., a 50 percent increase in the number of health facilities is required to produce a 25 percent decline in the morbidity rate.

Housing

Recent statistical and psychological research has indicated an inverse correlation between poor, overcrowded housing and the quality of mental health.[35] Other research, largely of a statistical nature, has suggested a comparable association with physical health. Among these studies are the correlation analyses of Lebowitz on Alameda County, California and Bedger on Cook County, Illinois;[36] a descriptive study by Wilner [37] presents convincing evidence of the same relationship.

In the present model, the impact of deteriorated housing on levels of health is presented through equation 1-75, suggesting that the slum environment has a generally deleterious effect upon health and that the incidence of certain specific diseases may be related to certain specific components of housing quality. An inverse curvilinear relationship (figure 3-11) between health and poor housing is posited. Change in this relationship is introduced from equations that determine

---

[b]The term "prefer" is used advisedly here. As noted, residents of urban ghettos frequently have little choice with regards to public health clinics versus private physicians, due to the limited supply of physicians and as a consequence of financial constraints.

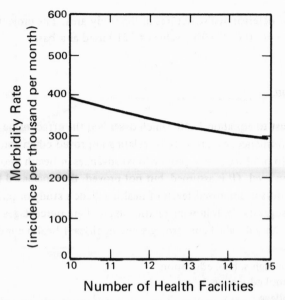

Figure 3-10. The Morbidity Rate as a Function of the Number of Health Facilities

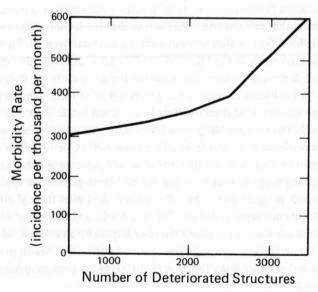

Figure 3-11. The Morbidity Rate as a Function of the Number of Deteriorated Structures

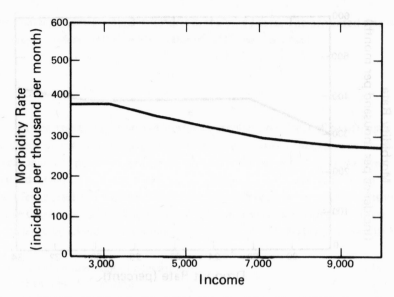

Figure 3-13. The Morbidity Rate as a Function of Income

The Income Submodel

Five variables were identified in the present study as critical to income levels in ghetto areas. These include age, education, and health—all forms of social capital—plus the more obvious economic factors of discrimination and employment (see table 3-3). The assumed interrelationships among these variables are shown in figure 3-14.

Age and Its Relation to Income

Studies by Becker, Singell, and Parker and Shaw [40] emphasize the importance of occupational experience (as reflected by age) to income levels. Becker argues that work experience is a form of social capital typically rewarded by higher wages. A study of urban labor force characteristics by Parker and Shaw reports that age is nearly half as important as education in determining the income level of an individual. Their analysis indicates that a 1 percent rise in job experience results in a ½ percent increase in income.

Similar results were obtained from a regression analysis of the data for the Miami Model City area. As shown in figure 3-15, the impact of age tends to increase slowly at first until age twenty-four; thereafter, its impact increases in

Table 3-3
Relationships in the Income Submodel

Income from: Independent Variable	Coefficient	Equation
Age	0.050	1-94
Education	0.300	1-100
Health	-0.160	1-104
Effects of discrimination	0.270	1-108
Employment	0.510	1-114

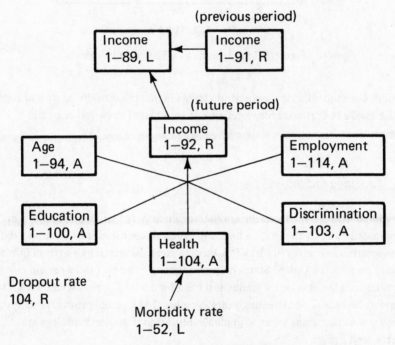

Figure 3-14. The Income Component of the System Model

a linear fashion. The relatively low level of occupational experience of the black (equivalent to twenty-four years) causes the contribution of equation 1-94 to be quite small. Change in the income level resulting from experience (age) is introduced in the model through a series of equations that duplicate the probable change in age levels in the study area. A base of 24.1 years is assumed. The rate of change applied in these equations is -0.004 per year or -0.95 over a ten-year

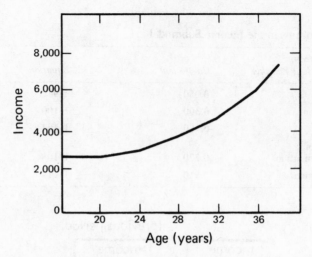

Figure 3–15. Income as a Function of Age

period. Consequently, the amount of change in income introduced by a change in age level as a surrogate for experience is anticipated to be rather small.

Education and Income

In contrast to the usual linear relationship between education and income expounded by most theorists, a highly irregular relationship is believed to exist between these variables in black low-income areas. Research by Harrison in ten ghetto areas in the United States indicates that earnings by blacks remain constant at a low level until graduation from high school, then increase in a stepwise fashion with increasing years in college.[41] Income rises especially rapidly with increasing years of graduate education. Harrison's findings are reproduced in figure 3-16.

These findings have a profound impact for equation 1-100, which relates the contribution (0.30) of education to income. Change is introduced through the education submodel; accordingly, the relationship is circular and permits exponential growth if unimpeded by independent or internal forces of the type described in chapter 2. Thus, the base dropout rate in the study are (28.8) need not imply an insurmountable obstacle to income advances. In theory at least, if the dropout rate decreases perceptibly, a marked rise in income should result. This circular-cumulative relationship is impeded in the model, however, by a

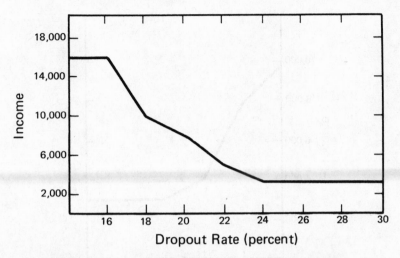

Figure 3-16. Income as a Function of the Dropout Rate

delay function (SMOOTH) that expresses a time lag to the impact of improved education on cultural attitudes.

Health and Income

Similar to the impact of health levels on educational achievement, there seems to be relatively little influence upon work productivity to be derived from decreased morbidity. Research by Albert *et al.* indicates that very few wage earners from low-income families miss work because of illness. In a sample of seventy-eight families, 93 percent reported one or more symptoms of illness per month. Of this percentage, symptoms were recorded for almost two-thirds of the children, one-half of the mothers, but only one-third of the fathers. Only 2 percent of the total symptoms were translated into requests for physician help or hospitalization.[42] The assumed nature of the relationship between health and income is depicted in figure 3-17.

Change in equation 1-104 occurs through data supplied by the health submodel. As a consequence of the peculiar nature of the relationship between these two variables, as given in figure 3-17, relatively little can be gained from advances in health levels (i.e., declines in morbidity rates) when these rates are between the 300 and 600 range. The greatest advances occur at the 100-300 level; however, even these gains, should they occur, are minimized by the comparatively small coefficient in equation 1-104.

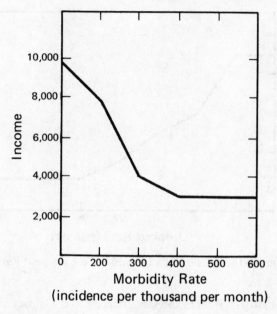

Figure 3-17. Income as a Function of the Morbidity Rate

Discrimination and Income

Apart from economic conditions, the single greatest effect upon income is racial discrimination. The effects of discrimination are widely documented. Myrdal and Becker, well known for their studies on social and economic discrimination, attribute nearly all the 30-to-50-percent salary differential between blacks and whites to discrimination. Social factors such as age, education, or health are considered of secondary importance.[43] This interpretation is reflected in equation 1-108, which gives a strong emphasis to the overt manifestations of discrimination in terms of salary differentials and labor force participation. These relationships suggest both the potential change in economic and social conditions of minority groups with the diminishing influence of discrimination and, perhaps, the fundamental difficulties in achieving such change.

Significant to this relationship is the declining effect of discrimination. Although statistical analyses of the type performed by Gwartney [44] suggest that discrimination in the labor market, in fact, is increasing, the bulk of the descriptive data—including studies by Northrup and Rowan [45] and by Ross and Hill [46]—indicate a slight relaxation of racial barriers in the job market.

These conditions, argues Hill, are reflected in the increasing number of blacks in sales, skilled trades, and the professions. This interpretation is incorporated in the present model through a steadily decreasing value of the impact of discrimination on income levels in equation 1-108, achieved through a series of rate and level equations.

Employment

Equation 1-114 reflects the widely held thesis that economic growth provides the main vehicle for the upward economic and social mobility of blacks. As the supply of jobs grows, a wider distribution of income results. According to Singell, "some people 'spill over' into affluence as income grows." [47] Conversely, as this supply declines, a smaller distribution of income results. Minority groups are particularly affected by the latter. Figure 3-18 depicts this relationship.

The model specifies a steadily increasing employment growth rate in the study area. A series of equations assign an annual increase of 0.029 percent to income levels as a consequence of increases in employment. Since the relation-

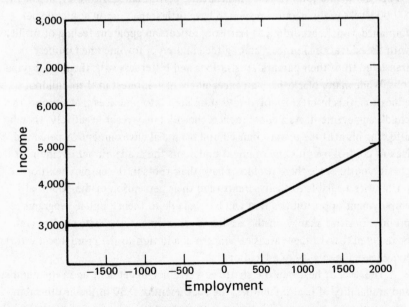

Figure 3-18. Income as a Function of Employment. *Note:* Employment is measured in terms of deviation from the number of jobs available in 1960.

ship between employment and income is strongly linear past the datum level (0.0) in figure 3-18, marked improvements in income can be expected. A partial delay function is included to reflect the unequal effect of economic expansion on minority groups. Singell reports that the incidence of poverty for nonwhite families will fall 5 percent less rapidly than for white families.[48]

Summary and Conclusions

Of the significant variables examined in the education submodel, those upon which public programs could conceivably have a direct impact—improved student-teacher relations, increased school facilities, advancements in teacher quality, and improved health levels—possess a lesser potential for effecting change than do those variables that are only indirectly accessible through public programs, i.e., student body quality, student economic background, and student family background. The findings of the Coleman Report that the attributes of other students account for far more variation in academic achievement of minority group children than any other factor is supported by the present analysis. In addition, the economic background of students accounts for nearly 16 percent of the total variance in academic performance. However, below the $4000 level family income appears to have little impact upon academic performance, which, according to Harrison, reflects an apparent feeling of futility with the educational process among the children of low-income families, translated from their parents' frustrations and bitterness with their low-paying jobs. While many blacks have an exceedingly high interest in their children's education, this interest is not always translated into practices that support the child's achievement. As a consequence, the child may react negatively, thereby affecting his attitude toward himself and his social environment. A perceived lack of control over his environment undercuts the academic achievement of the ghetto youth. Since these problems have their roots in the employment opportunities available to their parents (and their perception of the potential employment opportunities that will be available to them), public programs to produce positive changes in the academic achievement of ghetto students must be directed toward these areas of concern in addition to the more direct efforts to increase the quality of education.

The level of health in the ghetto is very much dependent upon the number and availability of health facilities; the coefficient of 0.30 in the health submodel suggests the importance of this proximity factor to a reduction of morbidity rates among residents of the study area. Increased awareness of good health practices (through education) can also contribute to improved levels of health.

However, since ghetto cultures often are reluctant to accept the different
behavior patterns that formal education suggests, persistent and forceful leverage
may have to be applied if the effects of health education programs are to be fully
realized. Rising income also plays a vital role in the reduction of morbidity
rates, particularly below the $6000 level.

Of the three submodels, income seems to have the greatest potential for
social and economic change. The exceedingly high coefficients associated with
discrimination and employment—combined with the peculiar nature of their
relationship to income, which implies a rapid rise in income with slight decreases
in discrimination or small increases in employment—suggest the possibility of
dynamic socioeconomic change. At the same time, these factors perhaps explain
the difficulty in achieving such change. The direct feedback loops to education
and health serve to accentuate the importance of the income submodel in
bringing about, if unimpeded, circular exponential growth in all three variables.

The study area can be characterized as a low-income area, its population
primarily black, with a relatively high potential for social disorganization—in
short, an urban ghetto. It can be perceived as a complex system containing both
positive and negative feedback loops. Without some type of external intervention into the processes of the ghetto, feedback loops with negative impacts
are likely to be predominant over time. External intervention in the form of
the Model City project, the Dr. Martin Luther King Boulevard Development
Corporation, or other public programs may provide the impetus to break
the "downward spiral" of negative feedback loops, and thereby provide the
opportunity for gradual influence of more desirable positive feedback loops. To
accomplish this positive dynamic change, however, it will be necessary to
identify further the key leverage points in the system. This, then, is the objective
of the next chapter of the study.

4

Model Simulation and Projections

The projections presented in this chapter are derived from a computer simulation model of the circular-cumulative relationship between education, health, and income for the study area. The format and arrangement of the model equations specified in chapter 3 are structured after those used by Forrester in his study of urban dynamics. In similar fashion, the format and theoretical bases of the model projections are drawn from the writing of Forrester on systems dynamics. In programming the model, the DYNAMO language was used (see appendix A). Unlike the more familiar programming languages, such as FORTRAN or PL 1, DYNAMO assumes an initial value for each variable and then works away from that value according to the relationships dictated by the estimating equations. With FORTRAN or PL 1, it is necessary to provide an array of incoming data to estimate the dynamic behavior of system. This requirement tends to be the greatest difficulty in using these programming languages in a dynamic context; in contrast, the relaxation of this requirement is the greatest asset of DYNAMO, and forms the rationale for its application in the present analysis.

Projections for each of the submodels—education, health, and income—are introduced first, building on the specifications outlined in the previous chapter. This discussion is followed by an examination of the estimates for the circular-cumulative model. The chapter is concluded with a further modification of the model through the introduction of the transportation variable.

Interpretation of Data Presentations

Estimates for each of the three index variables—education, health, and income—derived from the model for the period 1960 to 1970 are within a range of 1 to 10 percent of actual levels reported in 1970,[a] suggesting a fairly high level of validity in the modeling techniques. Calibration of the model to the

---

[a]Although the projected income figure is $600 below the actual average income for the study area in 1970, when adjustments are made for inflation (which averaged over 15 percent for the decade in the Miami area), the 1970 figure is closely approximated, resulting in a reduction of the range to 1 to 3 percent.

observed behavior of the ten-year period accounts for these highly accurate estimates. More important, at least theoretically, is the behavior of each component
over time. These behavior patterns are illustrated by tabular enumerations of
these variables. Each submodel was also depicted by the movement of supporting and index variables(identified by alpha characters) across the face of the
computer plots from the origin of the simulation at year 1960. The vertical axis
in each figure indicated time in annual increments, while the horizontal axis
represented the changing numeric quantity of the variables. From the origin, the
variables change in value, traversing the graph in a linear or curvilinear fashion
until the horizon year of 1970 is reached. Linear movement was shown as a
vertical plot on the diagram, as illustrated in figures 4-1 and 4-2. Nonlinear
movement was represented by a curvilinear configuration across the plot, which
may be either positive or negative in direction. If the movement was positive the
variable shifts (rises) from left to right on the diagram; if negative, the shift is

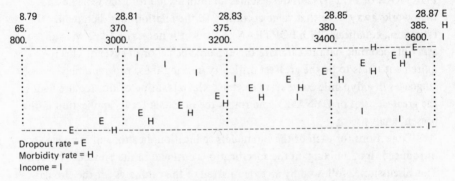

Figure 4-1. System Model—Education, Health, Income

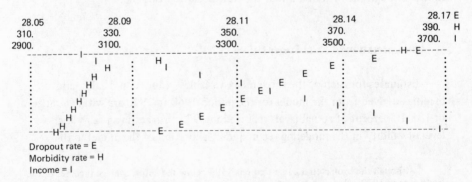

Figure 4-2. System Model—Education, Health, Income—with Transportation
Modifications

from right to left. This movement, of course, simply reflects the dictates of the estimating equations in the submodels. In interpreting system behavior, the use of these data plots provides a ready means of indicating the general type and direction of movement of component variables.

The second of the techniques used to analyze system behavior is illustrated by tables 4–1 through 4–3. Here the component variables are identified by name at the top of the listing, while the time interval (in years) is specified at the left of the tabulation. Actual numeric values, given by variable by year, occupy the separate cells of the matrix. Since the tables provide exact indications of component behavior, their primary application is to indicate the precise behavior of the submodel under consideration.

Education Projections

An examination of the data contained in table 4–1 suggests that the behavior of the educational component tends to be remarkably stable over time. The estimate of the dropout rate—the principal surrogate for aggregate educational achievement in this study—is within 3 percent of that actually recorded for 1970: the model projected this rate as 28.79, whereas the actual rate was 27.75. Thus, the projected dropout rate remained near its initial level, decreasing only 0.07 from the 1960 figure of 29.86. The eight contributing variables apparently failed to exert any significant effect upon the index variable (the dropout rate), as may be confirmed by an examination of these variables in table 4–1. The projected decrease in the student-teacher ratio (i.e., adjustments toward a more favorable ratio built upon the assumptions outlined in the previous chapter) failed to decrease the dropout rate at all during the ten-year period, remaining at its initial contributing value of 0.288, while the student-teacher-aide ratio declined only 0.001 from its original value of 0.433. Although the student-teacher quality ratio was set to advance quite rapidly during the ten-year period (i.e., significant increases in post-baccalaureate degree education among teachers were built into the model projections), these changes did not significantly reduce the dropout rate; a decrease of only 0.008 was evident. The three variables dependent upon the feedback loops from the income submodel—student body quality, student economic background, and student attitudes—also failed to contribute significantly to a change in the dropout rate. Combined, these variables decreased the rate by only 0.005, an amount less than that generated by the teacher quality ratio. Finally, the effect of improved health conditions, also dependent upon a feedback loop, was insignificant, remaining at the original level of 1.45. In short, the interdependency embodied in

Table 4-1
Education Submodel

	1960	1961	1962	1963	1964	1965	1966	1967	1968	1969	1970
Dropout rate	28.86	28.86	28.86	28.85	28.84	28.83	28.82	28.82	28.81	28.80	28.79
Teacher-student ratio	.288	.288	.288	.288	.288	.288	.288	.288	.288	.288	.288
Teacher-aide-student ratio	.433	.432	.432	.432	.432	.432	.432	.432	.432	.432	.432
Teacher quality	.547	.546	.545	.545	.544	.543	.542	.542	.541	.540	.539
School facilities	.489	.488	.488	.487	.486	.486	.485	.484	.483	.483	.482
Student body quality	2.30	2.30	2.30	2.30	2.30	2.29	2.29	2.29	2.29	2.29	2.29
Student objective background	4.52	4.52	4.51	4.51	4.51	4.51	4.51	4.50	4.50	4.50	4.50
Student attitude	4.92	4.92	4.92	4.91	4.91	4.91	4.91	4.91	4.90	4.90	4.90
Morbidity rate	1.45	1.45	1.45	1.45	1.45	1.45	1.45	1.45	1.45	1.45	1.45

Table 4–2
Health Submodel

	1960	1961	1962	1963	1964	1965	1966	1967	1968	1969	1970
Morbidity rate	382	383	383	381	380	378	376	374	373	371	369
Physician-patient ratio	38.8	38.8	38.8	38.8	38.8	38.8	38.8	38.8	38.8	38.8	38.8
Health facilities	114	114	113	112	111	111	110	109	109	108	107
Deteriorated housing	26.8	26.6	26.3	25.9	25.4	25.0	24.5	24.1	23.7	23.3	23.0
Dropout rate	46.9	46.9	46.9	46.9	46.9	46.9	46.9	46.9	46.9	46.9	46.9
Income	76.4	76.2	76.0	75.7	75.4	75.2	74.9	74.6	74.3	74.0	73.7

Table 4–3
Income Submodel

	1960	1961	1962	1963	1964	1965	1966	1967	1968	1969	1970
Income	3000	3028	3085	3146	3208	3272	3335	3399	3463	3528	3593
Age	150	150	150	150	150	150	150	150	150	150	150
Dropout rate	990	990	990	990	990	990	990	990	990	990	990
Morbidity rate	−451	−454	−453	−451	−448	−445	−442	−439	−437	−434	−431
Discrimination	810	834	857	880	902	924	945	965	985	1004	1022
Employment	1530	1565	1602	1639	1677	1716	1757	1798	1840	1884	1928

the model structure seems to inhibit any pronounced advances in system performance insofar as the education submodel is concerned. It would appear that without a very substantial increase in the more strategic system variables (as, for example, student economic background), other variables cannot be pulled upward sufficiently to modify total component behavior.

This failure to produce a more pronounced change in the dropout rate is probably related to: (1) the interaction between positive and negative feedback loops in several equations; (2) the curvilinear relationships that exist between the dropout rate and many of the contributing variables; and (3) the relatively slight advances in morbidity and income levels in the health and income submodels. With respect to the first of these influences, several of the estimating equations in the educational component were structured so that the functions were forced to vary under the dictates of the interacting feedback loops. In each of these equations, the positive and negative feedback loops were almost exactly balanced. As a result, the numeric value that entered the function was exceedingly low, causing a relatively small contribution of that equation to the index variable.

The second influence, that of curvilinear relationships, required that fairly significant advances in the contributing variable take place before a corresponding decrease would occur in the dropout rate. These advances were not achieved. Accordingly, even though some of the variables increased in an additive fashion, their eventual effect was minimal. Similar results were generated by the several feedback loops interconnecting the three submodels. An examination of tables 4-2 and 4-3 will reveal that the rate and amount of change in the health and income components were slight. The absence of sizable change, combined with the presence of curvilinear relationships, inhibited the potential contribution of feedback structures to the dropout rate.

Health Projections

Projections of the morbidity rate over the period 1960-70 were within 1 percent of the actual level reported in 1970. As shown in table 4-2, the estimated value was 369, just four points above the actual 1970 morbidity level in the study area of 365.

The behavior of the health submodel appears to be somewhat less fixed than that of the educational component. This pattern was also apparent in the data plots, which revealed that the curve for the health model is somewhat steeper, indicating that for the health component, the extent of system performance was greater and the pattern of that performance less rigid as compared to the education submodel. Nonetheless, this advance must be interpreted solely in terms of the behavior of the education component. The absolute decrease in the morbidity rate, in fact, was quite low. For the most part, it can be said that the levels of illness and mortality that characterized the study area at the start of the ten-year period were very much the same as those at the end of the period.

Still, the relative flexibility of this component should be examined. In the health submodel the effects of the contributing equations were somewhat greater, for they decreased the morbidity rate from 382 in 1960 to 369 in 1970. An examination of table 4–2 will disclose that the illness rate declined fairly rapidly at first, less so in later periods. This reduction must be attributed almost entirely to the effect of two variables. The projected increase in health facilities available to residents of the study area (from ten in 1960 to eleven in 1970) resulted in a 6-point reduction in the morbidity level. Similarly, the projected decrease in the number of deteriorated housing units between 1960 and 1970 (from 2100 to 1530 units), accounted for a 3.8-point reduction in the morbidity rate. Their combined effect contributed to a decline in the morbidity rate by almost 12 points over the period 1960–70.

The effect of the remaining variables was quite negligible. The physician-patient ratio, in fact, deteriorated during this period, dropping from 0.72 to 0.71 per thousand, reflecting a population growth rate in advance of the physician growth rate (possibly in combination with a further outmigration of physicians from the study area). The educational variable did not have any appreciable effect on morbidity rates. Although its estimating equations provided a small change, what little occurred was attenuated by the function in the model, which introduced a first-order delay into the feedback loop connecting the two models. Finally, the impact of the income variable was low. That feedback loop generated only a 2.7 decrease in the illness rate, from an initial contribution of 76.4 in the first simulation to a contribution of 73.7 in the second.

Thus, as before, the presence of the two feedback loops failed to exert an appreciable influence. Each was attenuated by their curvilinear relationship to the health variables and by their relatively scant advances in internal value. Lacking a circular-cumulative advance in certain variables, the health component was constrained in its development, depending entirely on the internally generated gains of its housing and facilities equations. Apparently advances of the latter type are not fully adequate to create a large downward movement in morbidity rates.

Income Projections

The projection of the income level (adjusted for the effects of inflation) was comparable in accuracy to the estimates made in the education and health submodel, being within 1.6 percent of the actual level in 1970. Table 4-3 gives the numerical values for the five equations in the income model. (The index variable is shown in constant dollars.)

The income component evidenced the greatest flexibility and largest gains over time of the three submodels. As a result of reduced morbidity and discrimination and increased employment, a fairly significant rise in family income was projected, from $3000 in 1960 to $3593 in 1970 ($4132 when adjusted for inflation). The data plot showed this increase to be sharply curvilinear, but tending to flatten toward the end of the study period.

This finding conforms to post-Keynesian macro theory, which asserts that income is inversely associated with unemployment but directly associated with advancing investment-savings and growth ratios.[1] Discrimination, which was stipulated to decrease by one index point over the ten-year period,[b] advanced the 1960 income level by $212. Employment, however, provided the greatest absolute contribution to income, improving the 1960 income level by nearly $400. The employment equations, it should be recalled, were formulated to reflect an expanding job market. The discrimination and employment equations in table 4-3 closely parallel one another, indicating that the relative contribution of each to the level is nearly identical, and that discrimination steepens somewhat toward the horizon year, suggesting that the effects of job discrimination are lessening even more substantially toward the end of this period.

Finally, the effect of the three social capital variables—age, education, and health—only contributed an extra $20 to income in 1970. An examination of table 4-3 will indicate that both age and education remained at their 1960 levels; only health evidenced improvement during this period. The effects of education upon income were ameliorated by a first-order exponential delay (SMOOTH) in the model; the nature of the curvilinear relationship between age and income stymied a contribution by that equation to income.

The insignificant impact of these three social capital variables seems to confirm the arguments advanced by Singell,[2] Becker,[3] and Myrdal [4] that economic advances for low-income minority groups must come from other, primarily economic, influences. Significant advances in health and education, they contend, will have little effect on income when discriminatory job barriers exist or when the labor market is experiencing decline or is stagnant. Nor will these variables have an appreciable effect on income when the job market is experiencing rapid advances, as in the late sixties, since the impact of discrimination is such that many jobs are denied to even highly skilled blacks. Seemingly

---

[b]The function in equation 1-108 received its value in terms of a deviation from a datum level, set at zero.

this argument is buttressed by the advances generated through the projected
reductions in discrimination and an expanding employment market, suggesting,
in turn, that public resources may be applied most effectively in the pursuit of
programs designed to reduce the legal-institutional barriers to employment.

Summary of First Model Simulation

Upon aggregation of these results, it would appear that the study area was
characterized by a high degree of stability. Only nominal change was projected
for the educational component, and only moderate change from the health and
income submodels. These findings conform to the actual situation in the study
area during the sixties. Little or no upward growth from its relatively low
equilibrium position was apparent during that period. Indeed some observers
maintain that the area actually declined in terms of performance toward reaching
broadly held community goals—improved education, better economic conditions,
and improved health levels. The general trend of the three components—education, health, and income—is given in figure 4-1. Note the nonlinear advances of
each and the gradualism of their increase. Actual numerical values are presented
in table 4-4. These projections, then, partially support Myrdal's theories of
circular-causation and circular-cumulative advance for low-income areas.

As pointed out in chapter 2, intrinsic to the process of circular causality is
an inextricable relationship of cause and effect that operates to imprison the
social or economic system in its own shortcomings: a given effect acts as a cause
to a substantially similar effect. The above data indicate that the Model City area
showed little advancement in the study period, and in fact remained in a state
of near equilibrium. Positive effects produced by contributing variables to
health, education, and income seemed negligible or nonexistent. Hence the conditions of the study area remained at initial levels, to produce generally similar
effects.

The concept of circular-cumulative advance was only partly confirmed in
this initial simulation. Change in one factor, say health, did not produce changes
of an additive type in other, related variables as suggested by a theory. There
seemed to be three reasons for this. First, in some equations the values entered
into the function were dependent upon the performance of linked negative and
positive feedback loops. Typically these loops were almost exactly balanced,
so that the magnitude of the numeric change was never great. Second, the
curvilinear relationships common to many variables suppressed a cumulative
advance in the numeric quantities of these variables. Third, the several feedback
loops interconnecting the three model components failed to generate cumulative

Table 4–4
System Model—Education, Health, Income

	1960	1961	1962	1963	1964	1965	1966	1967	1968	1969	1970
Dropout rate	28.86	28.86	28.85	28.85	28.84	28.84	28.83	28.82	28.82	28.81	28.80	28.79
Morbidity rate	382.00	383.89	383.32	381.97	380.29	378.53	376.76	374.99	373.23	371.47	369.72
Income	3000	3028	3085	3146	3208	3272	3335	3399	3463	3528	3593

change. According to Myrdal and other developmental economists, movement out of a low equilibrium condition—such as that characterized by an urban ghetto—cannot take place without the exponential growth made possible by these loops. Exponential delays of the type generated by the SMOOTH function exacerbated this circumstance. This consequence does not entirely invalidate Myrdal's cumulative theory, however. It may well be that very substantial advances in one or more component variables are necessary to push related variables past a cumulative threshold. Should these advances occur, the additive consequences postulated by Myrdal may eventually develop.

Model Projections: Transportation

The initial formulation of the dynamic systems model presented in this study presupposed that movement between residences in the study area and desired facilities generally was slow and highly dependent upon public transit. Modifications are now introduced to explore the impact of increased ease and convenience of such movements. These modifications correspond to improvements in accessibility made possible by a rapid transit system to serve the study area. Such a system is currently under study for the Miami-Dade County area.[5] Transportation modifications are estimated to be equivalent to a 40 percent reduction in travel time over the existing modes of travel; for the sake of simplicity, these reductions are assumed to occur in all directions.

The first step in the modification of the model to reflect an improved transportation system is to identify the appropriate revisions that, as a consequence, might be made in each of the submodels. These model adjustments include modifications to equation 1-36 to explore the effects of busing upon student academic performance, to equations 1-56 and 1-68 to examine the impact of increased accessibility to physicians and health facilities outside the study area, and to equation 1-108 to reflect greater potential accessibility to employment opportunities.

Education

The Coleman Report suggests that of all the attributes associated with the educational process (aside from student background and personality), the achievement of minority group children is mainly contingent upon the backgrounds, aspirations, and, perhaps most important, the work habits of fellow students.[6] Thus, equation 1-36 has been modified to reflect the presumption that exposure to the different values and work patterns of white children (achieved through the busing of black children to formerly predominately all-white schools) does, in fact, create a better attitude toward education among minority children. This assumption is incorporated into the education submodel by adopting a dropout rate of 20.0, which corresponds to the rate recorded in suburban Miami schools.

Health

Increased accessibility is assumed to lead to greater availability of physicians and health facilities in suburban areas to residents of the Model City neighborhoods. To reflect this factor in the health submodel, the physician-patient ratio was set at 1.10 per thousand, to correspond with a total urban accessibility to physicians, while the number of health facilities was set at 280 to achieve the same relationship. The improved accessibility expressed in these equations theoretically should result in a significant reduction of morbidity rates.

Empirical justification for these modifications—to buttress the descriptive evidence of such a relationship offerred by Salisbury and Robinson [7] and the statistical analyses of Hodges and Lubin [8] —comes from the high usage rates of a recently established health clinic at the center of the Model City area. Significantly, these usage rates—and evidence reported in other studies—correspond to the theories of physician utilization developed by Garrison. [9] According to Garrison, reductions in transportation cost should both increase the availability of physicians (and facilities) and decrease the cost of medical treatment. He explains the latter thus: "If the amount of services increase faster than demand in a given area (as it should when transportation expands the service zone for physicians) the price will fall." [10]

Income

Mass transit is assumed to have relatively little affect in improving income levels. As suggested by Kalicheck [11] and others, a fixed-route transit system is unable to provide the ready, convenient movement to suburban manufacturing and tourist trade industries required by central city workers. This situation seems to prevail in the study area. The dispersal of employment throughout the Miami area makes travel for the residents of the study area dependent on public transit very difficult, requiring multiple transfers and a considerable amount of time— often an hour or more. Model City residents apparently see these factors as significant obstacles; many elect to work in jobs close to their places of residence. The reduced regression coefficient, from 0.51 to 0.49, in equation 1-114 reflects this reluctance to travel long distances. (The relatively large number of families with cars—0.80 per family in the study area—ameliorates a more sizable reduction in this coefficient.) The difference in coefficient value was assigned to equation 1-108, which in effect reflects a form of economic discrimination.

Second Model Simulation and Projections

Once these new indices were determined, the initial computer program was modified to permit a second simulation of the model, incorporating the variable of improved transportation. The results, outlined below, were somewhat surprising in that, with the exception of the health component, changes in the accessibility to key facilities and opportunities by study area residents produced relatively few advances in total system performance.

Education Submodel

Modification of initial projections to reflect a more integrated school environment produced almost no change in the behavior of the education submodel. The dropout rate decreased by only 0.68 points from its original level of 28.6—an insignificant decline, given the magnitude of public investment involved in most busing programs. The fixity of the education submodel was documented by the plots of general component behavior (figures 4-1 and 4-2) and for the educational component itself. Comparison of the curves for education (designated E) in figures 4-1 and 4-2 will show that the general character of the educational component remained unchanged throughout both simulations. The shift to the right in curve E in figure 4-2 simply reflects the reduced dropout rate, not a major change in component behavior. The stability of the education submodel was even more perceptible in the data plots which depicted the behavior of each of the contributory equations in the submodel. The variable plots were nearly identical in both diagrams; curves H and P (health and student emotional background) evidenced a different arrangement, but in terms of *absolute* change the amount is minimal. According to table 4-5, which specifies the precise value of the education equations, health (H) advanced just .01 percent and student attitude (P) just .02 percent in the second simulation. Only equation 1-39, student objective background (O), demonstrated a real change between the two simulations, given in table 4-5, decreasing from 2.29 percent to 1.60 per-

Table 4-5
Education Submodel with Transportation Modifications

	1960	1961	1962	1963	1964	1965	1966	1967	1968	1969	1970
Dropout rate	28.16	28.14	28.13	28.12	28.12	28.11	28.11	28.10	28.10	28.09	28.08
Teacher-student ratio	.288	.288	.288	.288	.288	.288	.288	.288	.288	.288	.288
Teacher-aide student ratio	.433	.432	.432	.432	.432	.432	.432	.432	.432	.432	.432
Teacher quality	.547	.546	.545	.545	.544	.543	.542	.542	.541	.540	.539
School facilities	.489	.488	.488	.487	.486	.486	.485	.484	.483	.483	.482
Student body quality	1.60	1.60	1.60	1.60	1.60	1.60	1.60	1.60	1.60	1.60	1.60
Student objective background	4.52	4.52	4.51	4.51	4.51	4.51	4.50	4.50	4.50	4.50	4.50
Student attitude	4.92	4.92	4.91	4.91	4.91	4.91	4.91	4.90	4.90	4.90	4.90
Morbidity rate	1.45	1.44	1.44	1.44	1.44	1.44	1.44	1.44	1.44	1.44	1.44

cent. The abruptness and magnitude of that modification was reflected in
curve 0, which is linear, in contrast to the generally curvilinear pattern of curve 0
in the previous plot. Apparently the changes emanating from equation 1-39 were
incapable of forcing an upward movement in the educational component as a
whole.

As a consequence of the relatively small change in dropout rate resulting
from the new projections, the feedback relationships among the three models
failed to manifest exponential growth. In fact, the contribution of the educational component to these submodels, given in equations 1-40 and 1-100,
actually failed to generate any improvement in the health and income components. Examination of tables 4-6 and 4-7 will reveal that the education
variable remained at the 46.9 level in the health submodel and at the 990.0 level
in the income submodel. Delay functions and curvilinear relationships of the type
described previously impeded the long-term effects of these equations.

Health Submodel

In contrast to the preceding findings, the increased availability of physicians and health facilities made possible by transportation improvements
produced a fairly sizable reduction in the projected morbidity rate of residents
in the study area. This rate was reduced from 382.0 in the original simulation to
315.0 in the revised model, a difference of sixty-one points. The magnitude of
this change is suggested by a comparison of figures 4-1 and 4-2. In 4-2, the plot
of the index variable for health (H) is displaced toward the left of the diagram
and is only slightly curvilinear in its advance. In contrast, in figure 4-1 the path
of variable H is strongly curvilinear. An examination of figure 4-2 will also reveal
that the reduction in the morbidity rate was greatest in the first two years
(1961 and 1962), depicted by the sharp displacement of curve H to the left,
reflecting the assumed equivalence of the Model City health levels to corresponding levels of physician and health facility availability in the suburban
areas of Miami. Once past this early period, however, the morbidity rate declined
less rapidly (indicated by the near linear tract of variable H), although always in a
positive fashion. Apparently the effects of accessibility are greatest initially;
thereafter, they taper off as usage patterns are established and as people have a
decreased need for health services (as a consequence of reduced morbidity).

The impact of improved accessibility to physicians and medical facilities,
given in equations 1-56 and 1-68, upon the morbidity rate is suggested by the
changed pattern of curves P (physician-patient ratio) and F (health facilities)
in the data plot. Comparison of that diagram with the plot of the health com-

Table 4–6
Health Submodel with Transportation Modifications

	1960	1961	1962	1963	1964	1965	1966	1967	1968	1969	1970
Morbidity rate	302	335	325	322	321	320	319	318	317	316	315
Physician-patient ratio	21.0	21.0	21.0	21.1	21.1	21.1	21.2	21.2	21.2	21.3	21.3
Health facilities	84	84	84	84	84	84	84	84	84	84	84
Deteriorated housing	26.8	26.6	26.3	25.9	25.4	25.0	24.5	24.1	23.7	23.2	23.0
Dropout rate	46.9	46.9	46.9	46.9	46.9	46.9	46.9	46.9	46.9	46.9	46.9
Income	76.4	76.2	75.6	75.3	75.0	74.7	74.5	74.2	73.9	73.6	73.3

Table 4–7
Income Submodel with Transportation Modifications

	1960	1961	1962	1963	1964	1965	1966	1967	1968	1969	1970
Income	3000	3028	3163	3239	3305	3368	3430	3492	3555	3618	3682
Age	150	150	150	150	150	150	150	150	150	150	150
Dropout rate	990	990	990	990	990	990	990	990	990	990	990
Morbidity rate	-451	-376	-360	-355	-353	-352	-350	-349	-347	-346	-345
Discrimination	870	896	921	946	969	992	1015	1037	1058	1078	1098
Employment	1470	1504	1539	1575	1611	1649	1688	1727	1768	1810	1852

ponent for the initial simulation revealed that curve P after transportation modifications is not nearly as steep. This suggests that the physician-patient ratio is more effective in reducing the morbidity rate in the revised (second) simulation. A comparison of these plots for curve F disclosed an even more pronounced variation; before transportation modifications, curve F is generally curvilinear, whereas the same curve after modification is entirely linear. The linear track of variable F identifies a very substantial advance in the effect of medical facilities upon the morbidity rate. Indeed, the principal contribution to the reduction in that rate is generated from equation 1-68, which describes the influence of health facilities upon the index variable for health.

This reduction in the morbidity rate affected the education and income submodel differently. In the former, the contribution of health to education, given as the health variable in table 4-5, was slight, causing only a 0.01 percent reduction in the dropout rate. In the latter, its effect was much more pronounced. Improved health generated a $106 increase in income, an advance of nearly $86 over the original simulation. Much of this advance was produced during the early and middle periods (1960-64) of the simulation. After 1964, the contribution of equation 1-104 was less noticeable but still significant, as shown by the data in table 4-7. Seemingly, then, the effects of health are most pronounced as incomes rise and as the urban ghetto moves out of its low-equilibrium state.

The sharp increase in income from the reduction in the morbidity rate was the first instance of a strong exponential relationship between two submodels. These findings give partial support to Myrdal's hypothesis that advances in circular, low-equilibrium relationships can only be generated from sizable and across-the-board improvements in linked variables.

Income Submodel

Projected income levels showed little effect as a consequence of the revisions to the equations estimating employment and discrimination. The fixity of the curves for income (I) in figures 4-1 and 4-2 confirms the absence of significant improvement. To a very large extent, of course, this reflects the minor change in the conditions replicated by the two equations. Nonetheless it does seem that Kalichek's thesis regarding rapid transit and minority employment, at least, is partially validated.

A comparison of the data plots disclosed the main apparent reasons for the small advance in the income level with modifications in transportation. Two of the contributiong equations (age and education) remained unchanged, as indicated by the linear orientation of curves A (age) and E (education). More

Table 4–8
System Model—Education, Health, Income—with Transportation Modifications

	1960	1961	1962	1963	1964	1965	1966	1967	1968	1969	1970
Dropout rate	28.16	28.14	28.13	28.12	28.12	28.11	28.11	28.10	28.10	28.09	28.08
Morbidity rate	382.0	335.49	325.44	322.46	321.06	320.06	319.17	318.31	317.48	316.66	315.86
Income	3000	3028	3163	3239	3305	3368	3430	3492	3555	3618	3682

important, of the two equations that were altered—employment and discrimination—the magnitude of the resulting change was only moderate. The very
slight displacement from the pattern of the original simulation underscores the
relative absence of change in both employment and discrimination. Only health
contributed substantially to improved income, advancing the level by some $86.
The strongly curvilinear path of health, which contrasts sharply with the generally curvilinear path of that variable prior to modification, suggests that the
contribution by health to income was greatest during the initial rounds of the
simulation, from 1960 to 1963.

As a consequence of the relatively small change in the projected level of
income, the impact of the feedback relationships with the health submodel was
relatively slight. As shown in table 4-6, the health variable declined only 2.7
points (76.4 to 73.7) in the second simulation; hence change in the health
submodel was relatively insignificant. The stability of income confirms this
limited effect. Modification in the education component was obviated by the
changed format of equation 1-36, which set income to an artifically high level in
an attempt to stimulate the effect of middle-class conditions upon minority
group children. As noted previously, little change resulted from this modification.

Summary and Conclusions

With the exception of the health component, which decreased some
sixty-one points in the revised (second) simulation, changes in model accessibility
produced relatively few advances in total system performance. The dropout rate
and income level remained near their original (1960) state. Figure 4-1 depicts the
general trend of system behavior prior to the modification of the model; figure
4-2 shows the impact of transportation improvements upon this behavior. Note
the general stability of the education and income components, evidenced by the
generally similar track of variables E (education) and I (income) in the two
diagrams, and the absence of system fluctuations from the curvilinear movement
of the index variables. In a fully dynamic model, such as Forrester's *World
Dynamics*, the path of system variables are often oscillatory or highly skewed.
Only the health component (H) evidenced marked change, indicated by its
transition from a strongly curvilinear behavior in figure 4-1 to a nearly linear
movement toward the end of the study period in figure 4-2.

It is most significant that, of the three submodels to undergo revision of
their estimating equations, the greatest modification in these equations occurred
in the health component, which evidenced the greatest advance in system
performance during the 1960-70 period. Figure 4-2 shows this improvement

(curve H) to be strongly curvilinear at first, then almost linear in the later part (1963–70) of the simulation. The figures for the health variable in table 4-2 confirm the abruptness and magnitude of the change in this component. In this submodel, the two equations that had an important contributory effect upon the morbidity rate—indicated by the high coefficients assigned to these equations— were significantly altered: equations 1–56 and 1–68, used to estimate the effect of physician and medical facility availability upon the study area population, were reset to approximate an accessibility to these factors in terms of an efficient transit system. As a result of this change, a marked downward move- ment in the morbidity rate occurred, which in turn activated a positive feedback loop between the health and income submodels. It will be recalled that the health variable of the income component was instrumental in forcing the upward movement in the income level between 1960 and 1970. The fact that change was brought about in the previously low-equilibrium condition of the model suggests that: (1) system change can only come about through the revision of strategic variables, and (2) the change in these strategic variables must be large and operative over a relatively long period of time. Equations 1–56 and 1–68 were both modified to replicate an ideal circumstance and were both forced to operate for the ten-year period of the simulation.

Evidently, then, improvements in transportation do have a measurable effect upon system performance when there is a strong dependent relationship between the strategic variables of the system and accessibility. This effect is indirect, however, often expressed through the increased availability of an element critical to system behavior. Only certain of these variables are greatly dependent upon transportation for their effect, of course. Student attitudes, for example, which are vital to academic performance, are not related in any significant way to the benefits of transportation. In fact, most strategic variables are not dependent upon transportation to any great degree. Accordingly, the contribution of transportation to education, health, and income must be viewed in limited terms—as a catalyst or precondition to system change, but certainly not as the critical element of that change.

5 Sensitivity Analysis

The circular-cumulative model presented in this study has attempted to simulate the dynamic social processes of the Miami-Dade County Model City area for the period 1960–70, utilizing measures of education, health, and income to determine the overall level of variables within the model. The model theorizes that education, health, and income are related to one another in a cumulative fashion, i.e., an initial change in one variable is supported by consequential impulses in other variables, which give rise to repercussions, magnifying the initial change.[1] Thus, for example, it is hypothesized that additional units of educational attainment will contribute to additional units of health (reduced morbidity) and income, which in turn will contribute further to increases in units of educational attainment. The model does not, however, assume that equal amounts of education, health, or income will generate proportional levels of cumulative increase. Certain variables are more influential than others, and it is the purpose of this chapter to explore which of them are most influential.

The basis for this exploration has been established in the previous chapter. The circularity of the feedback loops in the model has been "tested" through the ten-year simulation. However, in complex systems, cause and effect seldom are closely related in either time or space. Feedback loops within such systems may be either positive (growth-oriented) or negative (entrophy-oriented), but the impact of these feedback loops may not be evident except over an extended period. Further, the actions of the positive feedback loops are not unlimited. The increment of change and the speed of response of the system act to limit the growth effects of the positive feedback loops over extended periods of time. Myrdal had identified three linked processes which also act to impede or retard the effects of positive feedback: independent counteracting changes; counteracting changes released by development; and time and inertia.[2]

To incorporate these factors into the present study and to identify the strategic variables in the model, a sensitivity analysis was conducted for the period 1960 to 1990, in order to measure the effects of incremental changes on the variables over an extended (projected) time period. The results of this sensitivity analysis should also provide a basis whereby variables that have the greatest potential for manipulation in order to successfully implement planned social change can be identified. Since the previous analysis of the model gave

81

evidence that the behavior of the level variables is fairly stable through time, without planned change, conditions in the study area will remain basically unchanged (or only slightly improved) through time.

The Methodology

Sensitivity analysis has been described as a means of measuring the possible effects of alternatives under analysis resulting from variations in uncertain elements. [3] In most problem situations, there are a few key parameters about which there is a good deal of uncertainty. Analysts faced with such situations must first attempt to determine a set of "expected values" for these parameters, as well as all other parameters. Recognizing that these expected values, at best, are "guesstimates," the analyst must use several values in an attempt to ascertain how sensitive the results might be (i.e., the relative rankings of the alternatives under consideration) in light of variations in the uncertain parameters.

In the present study, sensitivity analysis is applied in a similar fashion to determine which of the key variables are most influential in the dynamic change model. The horizon year of the analysis was set at 1990, with 1960 serving as the base year; it is assumed that all changes in variables occurred beginning in 1960 and continuing through 1990. Since the model was calibrated for the years 1960 through 1970, the possibility exists that projections may be in error as the horizon year is extended past 1970. The model does not consider certain exogenous changes that may occur in the study area, nor does it consider factors that cannot be quantified, either directly or through surrogates.

Changes of plus or minus 0.10 were made for each linked variable in the model. These changes were made in the relationship of the baseline (1960) to the projected (1990) value of each linked variable. In other words, the 1960 value of each linked variable remained unchanged; only the relation of the baseline value to the horizon-year value was manipulated. For example, the model equation for the physician ratio is HPHYRT = HPHRTP* (0.10), where HPHYRT represents the 1960 physician-patient ratio and HPHRTP* represents the projected (1990) physician-patient ratio. The equation means that the 1960 physician-patient ratio comprises 10 percent of the contributions of the health-related variables to the 1990 morbidity rate in the study area, through the 1990 physician-patient ratio. Assuming a plus or minus 10 percent variation, the manipulated values of this index would be 0.00 as the low value and 0.20 as the high value. This procedure was utilized in the sensitivity analysis in order to determine the potential for implementing change.[a] While public programs cannot directly change the dropout rate, for example, from 28 to 25 percent, they may be able to exert some effect on the influencing variables (e.g., school facilities) and on structural relationships (e.g., between health and education) which determine the dropout rate.

The basic model (the model with no manipulated variables) served as the data base against which changes in the manipulated variables were gauged. The manipulated variables were judged according to the degree of change that developed in the health, education, and income components (the level variables). The objective, of course, was to lower the dropout rate and morbidity rate and to increase the level of income.

The high and low values of each of the manipulated variables were utilized separately in the model. Computer trials were made with one manipulation of each variable per trial. After examining the results of these trials, certain of the high or low values of the linked variables that did not produce significant changes in the desired direction were omitted from further consideration. Manipulated variables which produced larger desired changes in the level variables (dropout rate, morbidity rate, and income) were then paired in order to determine the combined effect of their interactions.

Finally, all of the manipulated variables that produced desired directions of change were combined in one trial to determine the degree to which the model output could be changed under ideal (albeit unrealistic) conditions. Together with the results of the interactions within the basic model, this combination of all manipulated variables provides an indication of the widest possible ranges of values that could be achieved among the three level variables. Following the procedure outlined above, it became possible to identify the strategic variables in the model, i.e., those variables which are most influential in producing the desired directions of change in the components.

Findings

Following the first set of trials, it was found that one-half of the manipulated variables could be disregarded in further computer runs. Without exception,

---

[a]Certain of the variables were omitted from the analysis—student health, health from education, health from income, income from education, and income from health. These variables were developed specifically for the purposes of providing for feedback among the component variables in the model, and were omitted from the sensitivity analysis because they provide no "handle," that is, no means of being acted upon in the context of public programs for the Model City area.

these variables exerted an undesirable effect on at least one of the components and a neutral effect on the two remaining ones. It is of interest to note that these undesirable results were brought about by increases of all the associated linked variables of the education and health components and by decreases in values of all the associated linked variables of the income component. The manipulated variables that exerted a desirable influence on one or more of the key components, conversely, had low values for the linked variables of the education and health components and high values for the linked variables of the income component.

Education

As shown in table 5-1, the greatest change (a decline of 19 percent) in the dropout rate was exerted by the manipulation of student-body characteristics. Its effect on the dropout rate was much greater than that obtained from the next most influential educational variables—school facilities, teacher-aide-student ratio, and teacher quality—which all exerted approximately equal effects on the dropout rate (lowering it by 13 percent). Changes in the student-teacher ratio lowered the dropout rate by 12 percent, while the manipulation of the remaining two variables of the education component—student background and student attitudes—each decreased the dropout rate by 10 percent. With the exception of improved housing (which contributed a 1 percent reduction in the

Table 5-1
Effects of the Manipulated Linked Variables
on the Education Component

Manipulated Variable	Percentage Change in the Dropout Rate at Year 1990
Student-teacher ratio	-12
Teacher-aide-student ratio	-13
Teacher quality	-13
School facilities	-13
Student-body characteristics	-19
Student background	-10
Student attitudes	-10
Physician ratio	0
Health facilities	0
Housing	- 1
Age	0
Discrimination	0
Employment	0

dropout rate), the remaining manipulated variables had no discernible effect on the dropout rate.

Health

As shown in table 5-2, increased quality of housing exhibited the greatest impact on the study area's projected morbidity rate (a reduction of 32 percent). Housing quality is also the variable that had the greatest effect on all of the linked variables of all three key components. Its impact on all the morbidity rate was twenty percentage points greater than that of the next most influential health variable, improved health facilities, which decreased the morbidity rate by 12 percent. Changes in the physician-patient ratio lowered the morbidity rate by 9 percent, while decreased discrimination and increased employment opportunities had an effect of minus 1 percent on the projected morbidity rate. The remaining eight linked variables had no effect on the health component.

Table 5-2
Effects of the Manipulated Linked Variables
on the Health Component

Manipulated Variable[a]	Percentage Change in the Morbidity Rate[b] at Year 1990
Physician ratio	− 9
Health facilities	−12
Housing	−32
Age	0
Discrimination	− 1
Employment	− 1

[a]Education-related variables omitted since they produced no discernible change in the projected morbidity rate.
[b]Incidence of illness per thousand population per month

Income

The manipulated variable that had the greatest effect on the projected mean income level in the study area was again housing quality (see table 5-3). Its impact (an addition of 12 percent) was one percentage point greater than the next most influential variable. This finding is somewhat surprising, because housing quality is a variable in the health component of the model, and it might

Table 5-3
Effects of the Manipulated Linked Variables
on the Income Component

Manipulated Variable	Percentage Change in Mean Family Income at Year 1990
Student-body characteristics	5
Physician ratio	3
Health facilities	4
Housing	12
Age	6
Discrimination	11
Employment	11

have been expected that one of the variables in the income component of the model would exert the greatest influence upon the submodel. Proper changes in discrimination and employment both raised income by 5 percent. The remaining two linked variables of the health component, health facilities and physician ratio, raised income by 4 and 3 percent respectively. With the exception of student-body characteristics, none of the variables of the educational component had any discernible effect upon the projected level of income.

It is interesting to note that with the exception of the 5 percent increase in income exerted by student-body characteristics, none of the variables of the education component of the model had any effect on the morbidity rate or on income. Discrimination and employment had effects of only 1 percent on the morbidity rate, outside of their model component, income. The three variables in the health submodel all affected income, and of these, housing had a 2 percent effect on the dropout rate.

The effects of the variables in the health component of the model on the morbidity rate, on the average, were greater than the average effects of the remaining two sets of variables on their respective level variables. The variables of the income component had the least average effect on their respective component.

Paired Variable Analysis

A second level of analysis that can be conducted with these data is to determine the impact on the key study components of two linked variables acting in concert. When these combinations of changes in the manipulated linked variables were tested, a reduction of approximately 32 percent in the dropout rate was attained when the projected teacher-aide-student ratio, quality of teaching staff, and increased school facilities were each paired with student body characteristics. As shown in table 5-4, these were the most significant reductions in the dropout rate obtained by pairing the manipulated linked variables. Combining the projected teacher-student ratio with student-body characteristics resulted in a 31 percent decrease in the dropout rate, while a 29 percent reduction was obtained by combining student-body characteristics with both student background and student attitudes. Combining student background and student attitudes produced a 20 percent reduction in the dropout rate over the level projected from the basic model.

The combination of changes in accessibility to health facilities and increased housing quality resulted in the most significant reduction in the morbidity rate (43.4 percent) over that projected from the basic model. Pairing physician-patient ratio and increased housing quality resulted in a 41 percent decrease. When the housing variable was paired with the variable relating to discrimination, a 32 percent reduction in the morbidity rate occurred; similar reduction (approximately 32 percent) arose when the housing variable was paired with all of the education variables. It is significant that these variables did not affect the morbidity rate any more than the housing quality variable when it was unpaired. The highest reductions in the morbidity rate were attained when housing quality was combined with the other two variables in the health component. It is interesting to note that when housing quality was paired with each of the education variables and with two of the income variables, significant reductions in the morbidity rate were obtained, although these reductions were equal to the reduction exerted by the housing quality variable alone.

The impact of paired variables on income was not as uniformly patterned as was the case in both the education and health components. The largest increase in the projected level of family income (23.4 percent) was obtained when the housing quality and discrimination variables were paired. It is significant that this increase was below the percentage changes obtained when linked variables were paired in both the education and health submodels. A 21 percent increase in income occurred when the variables relating to discrimination and employment were paired. Pairing student-body characteristics and housing resulted in an 18.6 percent increase in income, while a 17.1 percent increase resulted from the pairing of age and discrimination variables. With the exception of student-body characteristics, when the education variables were paired with housing quality, identical increases in income occurred (12.4 percent).

The degree of change in level variables, when manipulated variables were paired, was not additive, as might be expected. This is due, of course, to the non-linear interaction of feedback loops in the model.

Table 5–4

Impact of Manipulated Paired Variables Upon the Three Model Components

Paired Variables	Component at Year 1990			Percent Change in Value of Component—1990		
	Dropout Rate	Morbidity Rate	Income	Dropout Rate	Morbidity Rate	Income
Basic model	27.981	309.06	$4721			
Student-body characteristics and						
(a) Student-teacher ratio	19.222			−31.3%		
(b) Teacher-aide-student ratio	18.934			−32.3%		
(c) Teacher quality	18.952			−32.3%		
(d) School facilities	18.919			−32.4%		
(e) Student background	19.835			−29.1%		
(f) Student attitudes	19.835			−29.1%		
Student background and student attitudes	22.229			−20.6%		
Housing quality and						
(a) Student-teacher ratio		211.06	$5306		−31.7%	+12.4%
(b) Teacher-aide-student ratio		211.06	$5308		−31.7%	+12.4%
(c) Teacher quality		211.06	$5306		−31.7%	+12.4%
(d) School facilities		211.06	$5313		−31.7%	+12.5%
(e) Student-body characteristics		209.84	$5599		−32.1%	+18.6%
(f) Student background		211.06	$5306		−31.7%	+12.4%
(g) Student attitudes		211.06	$5306		−31.7%	+12.4%
(h) Physician ratio		182.75	$5431		−40.9%	+15.0%
(i) Health facilities		175.06	$5456		−43.4%	+15.6%
Discrimination and						
(a) Housing quality		209.12	$5825		−32.3%	+23.4%
(b) Age (experience)			$5526			+17.1%
(c) Employment			$5734			+21.5%

88

Table 5-5 summaries the most desirable effects of both the single and paired manipulated variables on the key model components (level variables). It also provides a summary of the results of combining all of the manipulated variables in one trial. When all of the manipulated variables were combined in one trial, significant changes occurred in the level variables: the dropout and morbidity rates were lowered by 93 and 62 percent, respectively, and mean income was raised by nearly 138 percent.

Summary and Recommendations

This sensitivity analysis has shown that without the inclusion of manipulated variables in the model (that is, the absence of directed change), performance of the model as projected by the three level variables improves only slightly. When all of the manipulated variables are combined in the model, very significant changes occur in the dropout and morbidity rates and in income. In terms of the Model City project, this means that without directed change, conditions in the study area will continue as in the past, with only slight improvements. With a complete effort, however, significant changes can occur, and by the horizon year the study area should no longer bear the image of a slum.

On the basis of this sensitivity analysis, housing has been identified as the most strategic variable in the dynamic change model. An incremental change in the quality of housing can result in a significant reduction in the projected morbidity rate and a significant increase in the level of family income of residents in the Model City area. Other strategic variables have been identified and ranked in order of their influence on the three key components (level variables). Overall, the health component of the model was the most responsive to incremental changes in the base-year to horizon-year values of the linked variables. The income component was the least responsive to incremental changes in associated manipulated variables.

Of the education-related variables, student-body characteristics had the greatest effect on the dropout rate. Discrimination was the most influential of the three income-related variables analyzed. Neither of these two major variables, however, creates the large effects that housing quality produces with regards to morbidity rate or income. It is significant that an incremental change in housing quality has a greater effect on income than any of the three income variables investigated.

Only the health-related variables exerted major influences outside of their own submodel. The income variables exerted the least influence outside of their own submodel.

Table 5-5
Single and Paired Variables with Most Desirable Impact on Each of the Key Components at Year 1990

Variables	Level Variables at Year 1990			Percent change in Value of Level Variables		
	Dropout Rate	Morbidity Rate	Income	Dropout Rate	Morbidity Rate	Income
Basic model	27.981	309.06	$4721			
Student-body characteristics	22.640			−19.1%		
Housing quality		211.06	$5306		−31.7%	+12.4%
School facilities and student body characteristics	18.919			−32.4%		
Health facilities and housing quality		175.06			−43.4%	
Housing quality and discrimination			$5825			+23.4%
All manipulated variables combined	1.935	118.38	$11227	−93.1%	−61.7%	+137.8%

When manipulated variables were paired, greater desirable influences on the level variables were found. Depending on the goals of the various public programs that might be applied to the Model City area (or any other similar urban ghetto), appropriate combinations of changes in variables may prove beneficial. If, for example, the goal of these programs is to lower the dropout rate (and thereby achieve higher levels of educational attainment), the two variables to be manipulated most effectively would appear to be teacher quality (i.e., increase the number of teachers with advanced degrees) and student-body characteristics (i.e., increase the heterogeneity of students). Significant increases can also be anticipated from programs directed at the improvement of school facilities and student-body characteristics. If a significant reduction in the morbidity rate is the principal objective, public programs directed toward the increase of housing quality and the improved accessibility to health facilities would seem to hold the greatest promise of success. Similarly, if the goal is to provide the impetus for increased family incomes, the strategic variables upon which public programs might concentrate would appear to be those which would bring about improvements in the quality of housing and decreases in the incidence of discrimination. If the goal is to achieve across-the-board improvements in income, health, and education levels in the target area, the two most strategic variables upon which to focus public programs appear to be housing quality and student-body characteristics. Combining more than two variables, of course, would result in changes of greater magnitude than changes brought about through the application of paired variables.

The model is based on quantifiable data for which the appropriate disaggregated statistics were available. It is a well-known fact among census-takers that low-income areas present difficult problems in the collection of accurate data. The transient and anonymous nature of low-income areas are examples of major barriers to accuracy. It is also possible that the data utilized in this model may not completely mirror the dimension of the study area that they were intended to reflect. For example, the use of parents' income as a means of determining the impact of student attitudes on the dropout rate undoubtedly introduces unintended effects and biases into the analysis; but no better data than income appear to exist on an aggregate basis to reflect the dimension of student attitudes.

Not many of the total dimensions of human behavior can be quantified, and these subjective elements of behavior, such as attitudes and values, exert a great influence on behavior. Their exclusion from the model hopefully does not invalidate it, but the absence of unquantifiables must always be considered in any analysis of the model.

The model was developed on the basis of conditions in one small area within the entire Miami metropolitan area. The model incorporated only those variables which are internal to the study area. Exogenous changes, such as changes in the Miami economy and in the national economy, are not accounted for by the model.

Simple models are always desirable over complicated models. It is an unfortunate fact of life for the analyst, however, that the behavior that is being modeled frequently is not simple. It is the authors' opinion, however, that it is better to have some means of explanation and prediction, even though the model may have recognized shortcomings, than to be unable to explain and predict at all.

6 Conclusions, Model Evaluation, Future Research

At the outset of this volume it was noted that, while change is an ubiquitous characteristic of modern social systems, the impact of change is not uniform in all segments of a society. Change is not an isolated phenomenon, but rather, exhibits circular-cumulative patterns, whereby a change in one social variable may produce changes in many other variables, frequently with countervailing force. Inherent in this process is an extricable cause-and-effect relationship that may operate to imprison a social system in its own shortcomings. In short, a status quo may be perpetuated through a process of circular causation. Thus, to maximize the positive benefits of change for a given segment of society (and, by definition, to minimize the negative effects) requires a depth of investigation seldom undertaken in public programs for social experimentation.

Social change refers to significant structural alterations in parts or in whole social systems. Two basic and partially competing sets of theories have been advanced to explain social change. The first set of formulations focuses on the *nature* of social change—its magnitude, quality, kind, direction, and pace—endeavoring to explain it in terms of mutual relations that exist among elements of a society. The second set attempts to determine the dominant factors or *mechanisms* of change—changes in technology, social and economic institutions, and/or the values, attitudes, and beliefs of the society. Since aspects of both approaches are interconnected, difficulties often arise in empirical applications of these two theoretical spheres.

It has been the objective of this book to examine both the nature and mechanisms of social change, as they relate to an urban ghetto, through a simulation model developed to analyze the individual and aggregate behavior of three key social variables—education, health, and income. The model selected was patterned after Forrester's concept of "urban dynamics," while the theoretical framework was formulated from the concepts of circular and cumulative causation first developed by Myrdal. The circularity of the feedback loops in the model was first tested through ten-year (1960–70) simulations and then, in order to measure the effects of incremental changes on the selected variables over an extended time, through a sensitivity analysis conducted for the period 1960 to 1990. The objectives of these simulations were to clarify the dynamics of system behavior over time and to identify those variables that would seem to have the greatest potential for manipulation, in order to successfully implement planned social change through public intervention.

Conclusions

From the preceding analyses, a number of tentative conclusions, some already mentioned, have emerged concerning the structure and dynamics of system behavior in an urban ghetto. In large measure, these findings confirm Myrdal's theories of circular cumulative causation, i.e., initial changes in one variable may give rise to secondary changes that tend to move in an opposite direction, thus seriously hampering the positive aspects of the cumulative process. The stability of the low-income ghetto under study is readily apparent. System behavior over the ten-year period from 1960 to 1970 failed to show significant advances in the key variables. There was little evidence of oscillatory patterns in system behavior such as occur in fully dynamic and interdependent systems of the kind developed by Meadows and Forrester.[1] Neither did the simulation model evidence fluctuation about a mean equilibrium position, such as might have occurred with the balanced interaction of positive and negative feedback loops interconnecting the three model components of education, health, and income. Rather, there was a general fixity of model behavior, as indicated by the similarity of the data in tables 4–4 and 4–8. Thus it is apparent that Myrdal's theory concerning the permanence of low-income areas is substantially correct. The structure and processes of the urban ghetto tend to remain unchanged over time. The circularity of factors characteristic of such areas tends to preserve the status quo: a given effect acts as a cause to a substantially similar effect.

This analysis also confirms that the long-range impact of change upon the system is relatively slight. Change was introduced in the model through a simulated improvement in transportation (accessibility); with the exception of morbidity rates, which declined by some sixty-one percentage points, little change in system performance was evident. According to Myrdal: "If any attempt is made to lift any part of this mesh of interlocking circles (system), there is usually a downward pull so that any sustained progress becomes impossible."[2] This circumstance applies to the effects generated by transportation in this simulation; improved accessibility by itself cannot push the total system toward a higher level of performance. The circularity of other factors—health, education, and income—tends to inhibit the positive effects of change in a single system element.

While the inability of transportation to produce significant system change supports Myrdal's formulations of circular causation and low-equilibrium permanence, nonetheless a partial revision of his theory concerning circular-cumulative advance seems warranted. According to Myrdal, change in one factor in an interdependent system results in "consequential impulses, which in turn give rise to repercussions, magnifying the initial change." [3] The results of the second simulation indicate that circular change does not always lead to a pro-portional advance in other variables; in fact, it may not produce any change at all. In the present model, this phenomenon results from three programming structures: curvilinear relationships, delay functions, and small equation co-efficients. The curvilinear relationships peculiar to most variables act to minimize the cumulative advance generated by linked variables. Under this type of relationship, very substantial advances in numerical values would be required to produce a significant advance in bivariate associations. Delay functions and the relatively small equation coefficients tend to exacerbate the effects of many curvilinear relationships. The impact of these programming structures, then, is to minimize the cumulative advance in circularly related variables that Myrdal stipulates occur according to economic development theory. In short, the circular-cumulative advance that may be evident in underdeveloped countries does not manifest itself as directly in an industrialized society.

The foregoing suggests that, in order for cumulative change to actually take place, curvilinear relationships must be minimized and policy-induced change must be concentrated on those variables strategic to system behavior. Revisions of these variables, Forrester argues, transforms the performance of other system components, and eventually may lead to a cumulative advance in their behavior. [4] Hence, the theory of circular-cumulative advance, suggested by Myrdal, remains valid, but only within the context stated above.

The implications of system stability for planned change introduced through public programs should be readily evident. With respect to transportation, it appears that substantial improvements in the areal extent (coverage) and frequency of public transit service do not always lead to corresponding improve-ments in total system behavior, as is often assumed. Based on the results of the second simulation, which embodied modifications to further increase the availability of certain services to ghetto residents, it seems that transportation is a precondition and catalyst to system change, but not a determinant of such change. Although transportation modifications were introduced to each sub-model, a noticeable change in behavior was evident only in the health component.

The inability of transportation to induce such change stands in contra-diction to the formulations of locational economics and geography, which generally view accessibility as a dominant factor in dictating the location and density of land-use development. In contrast, the findings of the present study tend to support the formulations of several writers in the field of transportation planning. Creighton, for example, sees transportation as simply a mechanism to be used in obtaining broadly held community goals,[5] whereas Dickey views transportation as only one of the many determinants of the use of land.[6]

In fact, transportation tends to be a rather insensitive system parameter. Entered into several model equations, it failed to alter system behavior significantly. Apparently, for basic change to come about, there must be a fundamental revision of the parameters that exercise control over the system. According to Forrester, such parameters tend to occur at systems decision points; usually one or more of these points exists in each basic division of the system.[7] In industrial processes, these parameters—often called strategic variables—are situated at the policy-making level of the organization where issues are resolved concerning the manufacturing or distributional system, the administrative structure, and the future directions of organizational growth. These decision points are not readily apparent in urban systems; however, recent research indicates that they do occur amidst the economic processes of society. In the model discussed herein, these "decision points" were likely manifested in the discrimination and employment equations of the income submodel.

The following tentative conclusions can be specified regarding system change, based on why advances occurred—and did not occur—in the revised model:

1. In order to be effective, change must be induced through strategic variables; namely, those variables that contribute to and control system performance. In terms of the model developed here, these variables would occur within the income submodel as a consequence of the strong relationships between income and both health and education.

2. If the strategic variables cannot be identified with complete certainty, change must be introduced through a broad range of (what the planner considers to be) important parameters. The disadvantage of this approach of course is that, of the many programs developed to induce change, most will be relatively ineffective.

3. Change must be basic and operative over long periods of time; without sustained change, reversion to the original low-equilibrium state is typical, in accordance with the formulations of Myrdal. The failure of many otherwise feasible urban programs, such as the neighborhood health clinic program, can be attributed to the absence of an adequate and continued funding base.

Only when these conditions are fulfilled will the size and speed of variable response be sufficiently great to push the system upward, and only then will sustained feedback loops be activated. Experience has shown, however, that is is most difficult to completely satisfy these preconditions. Lacking any or all of these requisites to system revision, the basic structure and processes of the urban ghetto will remain virtually unchanged and near the low-level equilibrium, as was the case in the study area between 1960 and 1970.

On the basis of the sensitivity analysis, housing was identified as the most strategic variable in the dynamic change model, it was shown that an incremental change in the quality of housing can result in a significant reduction in the projected morbidity rate and a significant increase in the level of family income. Of the education-related variables, student-body characteristics had the greatest effect on the dropout rate, while discrimination was the most influential of the three income-related variables analyzed. However, neither of these major variables created the significant effects achieved by a change in housing quality.

When manipulated variables were paired, greater desirable influences on the level variables were found. Depending on the goals of the various public programs applied to an urban ghetto, appropriate combinations of changes in variables may prove beneficial (as noted in the conclusion to chapter 5). Without the inclusion of these manipulated variables—without planned change—conditions in the study area will continue as in the past, with only slight improvements. With a complete effort, however, significant changes can occur, and by the horizon year (1990), it was found, the study area no longer evidenced the image of a slum.

Model Evaluation and Future Research

Although the model presented in this study was developed in as accurate a manner as possible, there are nonetheless certain weaknesses in the approach. The first deficiency concerns the inadequacies of the simulation approach itself. Computer models generally are formulated about the interrelationships of a strategic set of variables, which may be very difficult to identify. Typically, the researcher surveys the literature, performs statistical analyses, and attempts by whatever means possible to identify the essential components of the system under investigation. Unfortunately, the search usually is confined to relationships that are quantitative, and as a result, important social conditions may not be identified or may be subsumed under the more quantifiable components. This perspective embodies obvious flaws. The analyst may fail to locate precisely the variables critical to system behavior; more important, he may fail to include critical social relationships as a part of the set of significant variable inter-relationships. To the extent that these approaches are followed, the simulation model will be of dubious merit. It should be evident, however, that great effort has been taken in the present analysis to identify the variables critical to education, health, and income relationships, and to include significant social components in model interrelationships.

Practical and conceptual difficulties may exist with the index variables—the dropout rate, the morbidity rate, and income. It will be recalled that the accuracy of the simulation estimates is very much dependent on the utility of the index variables in representing system performance. It may be that improper index variables have been selected, and that more appropriate measures of system performance could have been used. Still, great care was taken in selecting these variables, and without exception these measures are used by authorities in the fields of education, health, and economics.

It is questionable if the proper spatial boundaries were chosen for the study area. Although an attempt was made to define the areas of the ghetto community through research of census and local planning agency data and through conversations with planning officials knowledgeable of the area, the possibility exists that important factors delimiting the boundaries of the community were not included in this analysis. This shortcoming may be especially evident in the areas to the north and west of the study area, where there has been a dispersal of ghetto residents in the past few years. Groups living in these areas may still think of themselves as part of the ghetto community, and may still have close ties in terms of social and economic relationships. Failure to include these areas in the analysis, therefore, may mean that the equations and feedback relationships are not precisely matched to the actual conditions of the total community —with attendant consequences to the subsequent simulation estimates.

Related to the previous criticism is the failure of this model to include the possible effects of exogenous variables. Events are frequently controlled not by local conditions but by external influences; economic and political decisions made at the regional and national level may well have a significant effect on local actions. (A decision by a New York investor to build a manufacturing plant near the Model City area is an example of an exogenous or external influence.) Unfortunately there is no current way to predict the occurrence of these influences, much less forecast the exact repercussions of their effect. Accordingly, to the extent that the exogenous variables influence the behavior of the study area, the simulation model lacks precision.

Finally, it may be that the simulation model is not fully geared to the dynamics of the Model City area. The equations in the model were based on segmental cuts of time series data, and while an attempt was made to calibrate the model with known change, it may be that this attempt was not wholly successful. A more dynamic modeling approach may be required to capture the full characteristics of systems performance. Problems of time and data availability, however, would probably forestall such an analysis, given the present state of the art.

Future research could profitably concentrate on the difficulties described above, should the model be found deficient in these respects. Other avenues of potential research include the enlargement of the model to reflect a wide range of system relationships and the development of a holistic model to include the estimates generated by this present model as subroutines. It would prove extremely valuable to simulate the urban ghetto as a wholly interdependent system. This approach implies the inclusion of many more interrelationships to replicate fully the conditions of the urban ghetto over time. Current knowledge of interdependent social, economic, and behavioral processes in urban ghettos is scant. Inclusion of the model developed herein as part of a more comprehensive simulation program would eliminate the need to develop equations in the fields of health, education, and income, thereby permitting research efforts to be devoted to other areas.

In the conclusion to chapter 1, a number of questions were raised concerning the need for new mechanisms to provide urban systems with better adaptability to change. While this study has not provided definitive answers to these questions, it is hoped that this research will encourage others to investigate the linked processes of the urban ghetto as a means of developing such responses. As a field that attempts to develop and implement workable programs for social change, it is essential that the dynamics of such areas of the urban system be understood by public planners. It may be suggested that the simulation technique provides a particularly effective method for analysing such processes. It can be especially effective in relating the social and economic dynamics of the ghetto to the conditions of the larger metropolitan area. It is hoped that the model developed here may provide a point of departure for such further research.

Appendix A
Circular Cumulative Model

```
CIRCULAR CUMULATIVE MODEL. INCOME EDUC HEALTH    12/05/72

* CIRCULAR CUMULATIVE MODEL. INCOME EDUC HEALTH
NOTE EDUCATION SUBMODEL
L EDUC.K=EDUC.J+DT*(REA.JK-REO.JK)
N EDUC=5160
R REA.KL=EDUC.K*(.29)
R REO.KL=(DROP.K*.01)*EDUC.K
A DROP.K=TE.K+DROPSF.K+DROPSQ.K+DROPSB.K+DROPSA.K+DROPH.K+RANDOM
A TE.K=DROPTS.K+DROPTA.K+DROPTQ.K
NOTE STUDENT TEACHER RATIO
A DROPTS.K=DRPTS.K*.01
A DRPTS.K=TABLE(RDRTS,STCHG.K,22,32,1)
T RDRTS=28.0/28.2/28.4/28.6/28.8/28.8/28.8/28.9/30.0/30.2/30.3
A STCHG.K=ST.K/TK.K
L ST.K=ST.J+DT*RST.JK
N ST=5160
R RST.KL=ST.K*(.029)
L TK.K=TK.J+DT*RTK.JK
N TK=178
R RTK.KL=TK.K*(.03)
NOTE STUD. TAIDE RATIO
A DROPTA.K=DRPTA.K*(.015)
A DRPTA.K=TABLE(RDRTS,STTACG.K,22,32,1)
A STTACG.K=ST.K/TKTA.K
A TKTA.K=TK.K+TA.K
L TA.K=TA.J+DT*(RTA.JK)
N TA=2
R RTA.KL=TA.K*(.05)
NOTE TEACHER QUALITY
A DROPTQ.K=DRPTQ.K*(.019)
A DRPTQ.K=TABLE(RDRTQ,TEL.K,16,18,.5)
T RDRTQ=28.8/28.6/28.4/27.8/27.0
L TEL.K=TEL.J+DT*(RTEL.JK)
N TEL=16.0
R RTEL.KL=TEL.K*(.006)
NOTE SCHOOL FACILITIES
A DROPSF.K=DRSF.K*(.017)
A DRSF.K=TABLE(RDSF,SF.K,10,14,1)
T RDSF=28.8/28.4/28.2/28.1/28.0
L SF.K=SF.J+DT*RSF.JK
N SF=10
R RSF.KL=SF.K*(.01)
NOTE STUDENT BODY QUALITY
A DROPSQ.K=DRSQ.K*(.08)
A DRSQ.K=TABLE(RDSQ,EI.K,1000,9000,1000)
T RDSQ=28.8/28.8/28.8/28.6/28.0/27.2/26.5/25.7/25.0
NOTE STUDENT OBJECTIVE BACKGROUND
A DROPSB.K=DRSB.K*(.157)
A DRSB.K=TABLE(RDSB,EI.K,1000,9000,1000)
T RDSB=28.8/28.8/28.8/28.6/28.0/27.2/26.5/25.7/25.0
A EI.K=INCOME.K*(1.0)
```

```
NOTE STUDENT ATTITUDES
A DROPSA.K=DRSA.K*(.171)
A DRSA.K=TABLE(RDSA,EI.K,1000,9000,1000)
T RDSA=28.8/28.8/28.8/28.6/28.0/27.2/26.5/25.7/25.0
NOTE EFFECT OF HEALTH
A DROPH.K=DRHP.K*(.05)
A DRHP.K=TABLE(RDRHP,EH.K,0,600,100)
T RDRHP=28.0/28.2/28.4/28.8/29.2/30.5/32.0
```

CIRCULAR CUMULATIVE MODEL. INCOME EDUC HEALTH   12/05/72

```
A  EH.K=HEALTH.K*(1.0)
NOTE EFFECT OF OTHER VARIABLES
C  RANDOM=13.9
NOTE HEALTH SUBMODEL
L  HEALTH.K=HEALTH.J+DT*(RHS.JK-RHA.JK)
N  HEALTH=382
R  RHA.KL=HEALTH.K
R  RHS.KL=HPHYRT.K+HFACS.K+HH.K+HEDUC.K+HINC.K+RADMNH.K
NOTE PHYSICIAN RATIO
A  HPHYRT.K=HPHRTP.K*(.10)
A  HPHRTP.K=TABHL(RHPP,DOCPOP.K,.50,1.20,.10)
T  RHPP=410/400/390/380/350/310/270/210
A  DOCPOP.K=DIFDP.K-TRANSH
A  DIFDP.K=(DOCGR.K/POPGR.K)/.001
C  TRANSH=.48
L  DOCGR.K=DOCGR.J+DT*(RDOCGR.JK)
N  DOCGR=1200
R  RDOCGR.KL=DOCGR.K*(.0295)
L  POPGR.K=POPGR.J+DT*(RPOPGR.JK)
N  POPGR=1000000.00
R  RPOPGR.KL=POPGR.K*(.03)
NOTE HEALTH FACILITIES
A  HFACS.K=HFACSP.K*(.30)
A  HFACSP.K=TABLE(RHFP,FAC.K,10,15,1)
T  RHFP=382/360/340/320/300/280
L  FAC.K=FAC.J+DT*(RFAC.JK)
N  FAC=10.0
R  RFAC.KL=FAC.K*(.01)
NOTE HOUSING
A  HH.K=HOUSIN.K*(.07)
A  HOUSIN.K=TABHL(RHOP,RHO.K,50,350,50)
T  RHOP=300/320/325/380/400/500/600
L  RHO.K=RHO.J+DT*(RRHO.JK)
N  RHO=210
R  RRHO.KL=RHO.K*(-.031)
NOTE EFFECT OF EDUCATION
A  HEDUC.K=HEDUCP.K*(.123)
A  HEDUCP.K=TABLE(RHEP,HE.K,18,34,2)
T  RHEP=300/360/382/382/382/382/382/400/420
A  HE.K=DROP.K*(1.0)
NOTE INCOME
A  HINC.K=HINCP.K*(.20)
A  HINCP.K=TABLE(RINC,HI.K,2000,9000,1000)
T  RINC=382/382/360/340/325/300/280/270
A  HI.K=INCOME.K
A  RADMNH.K=HEALTH.K*(.21)
NOTE INCOME SUBMODEL
L  INCOME.K=INCOME.J+(DT)*(RIO.JK-RIA.JK)
N  INCOME=3000
R  RIA.KL=INCOME.K
R  RIO.KL=INCSOC.K+INCOSM.K+INCEMP.K
NOTE SOCIAL CAPITAL
A  INCSOC.K=INCAGE.K+INCED.K+INCHLT.K
NOTE AGE
A  INCAGE.K=INCAGP.K*(.05)
A  INCAGP.K=TABLE(RIAP,AVAGE.K,16,36,2)
T  RIAP=2800/2800/2800/3000/3000/3400/3900/4200/4800/5100/5800
L  AVAGE.K=AVAGE.J+DT*(RAVAGE.JK)
```

```
CIRCULAR CUMULATIVE MODEL. INCOME EDUC HEALTH    12/05/72

N AVAGE=24.0
R RAVAGE.KL=AVAGE.K*(-.004)
NOTE EDUCATION
A INCED.K=INCEDP.K*(.33)
A INCEDP.K=TABLE(RAVINE,SMOOTH(IE.K,.5),12,30,2)
T RAVINE=16000/16000/16000/10000/8000/4200/3000/3000/3000/3000
A IE.K=DROP.K*(1.0)
NOTE HEALTH
A INCHLT.K=INCHTP.K*(-.16)
A INCHTP.K=3000+(3000-INCHMP.K)
A INCHMP.K=TABLE(RIHP,HHLT.K,100,600,100)
T RIHP=10000/8000/4000/3000/3000/3000
A HHLT.K=HEALTH.K*(1.0)
NOTE DISCRIMINATION
A INCDSM.K=INCDRP.K*(.27)
A INCDRP.K=TABLE(RIDP,DISM.K,0,10,2)
T RIDP=6000/5400/4000/3000/3000/3000
L DISM.K=DISM.J+DT*(RDISM.JK)
N DISM=6.0
R RDISM.KL=DISM.K*(-.03)
NOTE EMPLOYMENT
A INCEMP.K=INCEP.K*(.51)
A INCEP.K=TABHL(RIED,EMPOP.K,486,6486,1000)
T RIED=3000/3000/3000/3000/3800/4000/5000
L EMPOP.K=EMPOP.J+DT*(PEMPOP.JK)
N EMPOP=3486
R REMPOP.KL=EMPOP.K*(.025)
NOTE DIRECTION CARDS
PRINT EDUC,REA,REO,DRCP,DROPTS,STCHG,ST,TK,DROPTA,STTACG,TA,DROPTQ,TEL
PRINT DROPSF,SF,DROPSQ,DROPSB,EI,DROPSA,DROPH,EH
PRINT HEALTH,RHA,RHS,HPHYRT,DOCPOP,DOCGR,POPGR,HFACS,FAC,HH,RHO,HEDUC,I
PRINT HINC,HI
PRINT INCOME,RIA,RIO,INCSOC,INCAGE,AVAGE,INCED,IE,INCHLT,HHLT,INCDSM
PRINT DISM,INCEMP,EMPOP,REMPOP
PLOT  DROP=E/DROPTS=T/DROPTA=A/DROPTQ=Q/DROPSF=F/DROPSQ=O/DROPSB=B
PLOT  DROPSA=P/DROPH=H
PLOT  HEALTH=H/HPHYRT=P/HFACS=F/HH=S/HEDUC=E/HINC=I
PLOT  INCOME=I/INCSOC=S/INCAGE=A/INCED=E/INCHLT=H/INCDSM=D/INCEMP=J
PLOT  DROP=E/HEALTH=H/INCOME=I
SPEC  DT=1.0/LENGTH=10.0/PRTPER=1.0/PLTPER=1.0
RUN   BASIC MODEL
```

Appendix B
Definition of Terms

Education Submodel

DROPTS.K = DRPTS.K * (0.01)   1-7, A

DROPTS   Dropout rate from teacher-student ratio
DRPTS   Dropout rate from teacher-student ratio, projected

DROPTA.K = DRPTA.K * (.015)   1-17, A

DROPTA   Dropout rate from teacher-aide-student ratio
DRPTA   Dropout rate from teacher-aide-student ratio, projected

DROPTQ.K = DRPTQ.K * (.019)   1-24, A

DROPTQ   Dropout rate from teacher quality
DRPTQ   Dropout rate from teacher quality, projected

DROPSF.K = DRSF.K * (.017)   1-30, A

DROPSF   Dropout rate from number of school facilities
DRSF   Dropout rate from number of school facilities, projected

DROPSQ.K = DRSQ.K * (.080)   1-36, A

DROPSQ   Dropout rate from student body quality
DRSQ   Dropout rate from student body quality, projected

DROPSB.K = DRSB.K * (.157)   1-39, A

DROPSB   Dropout rate from student background
DRSB   Dropout rate from student background, projected

DROPSA.K = DRSA.K * (.171)   1-43, A

DROPSA   Dropout rate from student attitudes
DRSA   Dropout rate from student attitudes, projected

DROPH.K = DRHP.K * (.05)   1-46, A

DROPH   Dropout rate from health
DRHP   Dropout rate from health, projected

Health Submodel

HPHYRT.K = HPHRTP.K * (.10)   1-56, A

HPHYRT   Health from physician-patient ratio

HPHRTP   Health from physician-patient ratio, projected

HFACS.K = HFACSP.K * (.30)   1-68, A
HFACS   Health from number of facilities
HFACSP   Health from number of facilities, projected

HH.K = HOUSIN.K * (.07)   1-75, A
HH   Health from housing
HOUSIN   Health from housing, projected

HEDUC.K = HEDUCP.K * (.123)   1-81, A
HEDUC   Health from education
HEDUCP   Health from education, projected

HINC.K = HINCP.K * (.20)   1-84, A
HINC   Health from income
HINCP   Health from income, projected

Income Submodel

INAGE.K = INACP.K * (.05)   1-94, A
INAGE   Income from age
INCACP   Income from age, projected

INCED.K = INCEDP.K * (.30)   1-100, A
INCED   Income from education
INCEDP   Income from education, projected

INCHLT.K = INCHTP.K * (-.16)   1-104, A
INCHLT   Income from health
HCHTP   Income from health, projected

INCDSM.K = INCDSP.K * (.27)   1-108, A
INCDSM   Income from effects of discrimination
INCDSP   Income from effects of discrimination, projected

INCEMP.K = INCEP.K * (.51)   1-114, A
INCEMP   Income from employment
INCEP   Income from employment, projected

Notes

Chapter 1
Social Change in Urban Society

1. Norman F. Washburne, *Interpreting Social Change in America* (Garden City: Doubleday, 1954).
2. Jay W. Forrester, *Industrial Dynamics* (Cambridge: MIT Press, 1961); *Urban Dynamics* (Cambridge: MIT Press, 1969); *World Dynamics* (Cambridge: Wright-Allen Press, 1971); and *Principles of Systems* (Cambridge: Wright-Allen Press, 1972).
3. For a further discussion of this distinction, *see* Wilbert E. Moore, *Man, Time and Society* (New York: John Wiley & Sons, 1963).
4. Lewis H. Morgan, *Ancient Society* (New York: C.H. Kerr, 1907).
5. F. Stuart Chapin, *Cultural Change* (New York: D. Appleton-Century, 1928), pp. 207-14.
6. Robert L. Sutherland and Julian L. Woodward, *Introductory Sociology* (New York: Lippincott, 1948), p. 747.
7. Pitirim Sorokin, *Social and Cultural Dynamics*, Vol. 1 (New York: American Book Company, 1937), pp. 186ff.
8. William F. Ogburn, *Social Change* (New York: B.W. Heubsch, 1922).
9. Jiri Musil, "Models of Growth and Change in Society," *Ekistics* (November 1970), p. 364. The authors are indebted to Musil for his compilation of various models discussed herein.
10. John W. Kendrick, *Productivity Trends: Capital and Labor* (Princeton: Princeton University Press, 1956).
11. Wilbert E. Moore, *Social Change* (Englewood Cliffs: Prentice Hall, 1963).
12. Lewis Mumford, *Technics and Civilization* (New York: Harcourt, Brace, 1933).
13. Musil, *op. cit.*, p. 365.
14. Forrester, *op. cit.* (1971).
15. David Bayliss, *Some Recent Trends in Forecasting* (London: Center for Environmental Studies, Working Paper #17, 1968); Hornell Hart, "Social Theory and Social Change," in *Symposium on Sociological Theory*, edited by Llewellyn Gross (Evanston: Row Peterson, 1959); M.J.H. Mogridge, "The Prediction of Car Ownership," *Journal of Transport Economics and Policy*, Vol. 1 (January 1967).
16. Ernest M. Burgess, "The Concept of Personal Adjustment," in Ruth S. Cavan, *et. al.*, (Chicago: University of Chicago Press, 1949).
17. The best-known conflict theories are those developed by Marx, Simmel, Gumplowicz, Novikov, and Ratzenhofer. For a modern interpretation of

conflict theory, *see* Lewis A. Coser, *The Functions of Social Conflict* (London: Routledge Press, 1956).

18. William F. Cottrell, "Death by Dieselization: A Case Study in the Reaction to Technological Change," *American Sociological Review*, Vol. 16 (1951), pp. 358–65.

19. Percy S. Cohen, *Modern Social Theory* (London: Heinemann, 1968), p. 203.

20. Ogburn, *op. cit.*

21. Philip Hauser (ed.), "World Urbanism," *American Journal of Sociology*, Vol. 60 (March 1955), entire issue.

22. "Modeles d'Urbanisation," Institut d'Aménagement et d'Urbanisme de la Région Parisienne (Paris: 1968).

23. Ira S. Lowry, "A Short Course in Model Design," in *Spatial Analysis: A Reader in Statistical Geography*, edited by Brian J.L. Berry and Duane F. Marble (Englewood Cliffs: Prentice-Hall, 1968), pp. 53–64.

24. For a further discussion of these early models, *see* Alan Walter Steiss, *Models for the Analysis and Planning of Urban Systems* (Lexington, Mass.: Lexington Books, D.C. Heath, 1974), chapter 4.

25. Lowdon Wingo, "An Economic Model for the Utilization of Urban Land," Regional Science Association Papers and Proceedings, Vol. 7 (1961).

26. John F. Kain, *A Contribution to the Urban Transportation Debate: An Economic Model of Urban Residential and Travel Behavior* Santa Monica: Rand Corporation, 1962).

27. Lowry, *op. cit.*, p. 54.

28. The foundations of the Penn-Jersey model are to be found in the study by John D. Herbert and Benjamin Stevens ("A Model for the Distribution of Residential Activity in Urban Areas," *Journal of Regional Science Association*, Vol. 2 [1960]); the model was then developed further by Britton Harris (*Basic Assumptions for a Simulation of the Urban Residential Housing and Land Market* [Philadelphia: University of Pennsylvania, 1966]).

29. George T. Lathrop and J.R. Hamburg, "Opportunity-Accessibility Model for Allocating Regional Growth," *Journal of the American Institute of Planners*, Vol. 31 (1965), pp. 95–103; E.R. Brigham, *A Model of Residential Land Values* (Santa Monica: Rand Corporation, 1964); Ira S. Lowry, *A Model of Metropolis* (Santa Monica: Rand Corporation, 1964).

30. Roy E. Pahl, *Readings in Urban Sociology* (New York: Pergamon Press, 1968).

31. Lowry, *op. cit.* (1968), p. 55.

32. John Dickey, "Minimizing Economic Segregation Through Transit System Changes: A Goal Programming Approach," *Traffic Flow and Transportation*, edited by Gordon F. Newell (New York: American Elsevier, 1972), pp. 57–108.

33. Martin Shubik, "Simulation of Socio-Economic Systems. Part II: An Aggregative Socio-Economic Simulation of a Latin American Country," in *Contemporary Sociological Theory*, edited by Fred E. Katz (New York: Random House, 1971), pp. 277–309.

34. Peter Haggett, *Locational Analysis in Human Geography* (London: Edward Arnold, 1965), pp. 29–169.

35. John W. Dickey and R.A. Hall, "Experiments with an Interactive Search Procedure for Changing Transportation to Guide Urban Growth" (Virginia Tech Department of Civil Engineering, 1971), mimeographed; Dickey, *op. cit.* (1972); John W. Dickey, *et al.,* "Use of TOPAZ for Generating Alternate Land Use Schemes" (Virginia Tech Division of Environmental and Urban Systems, 1971), mimeographed; Britton Harris, *Basic Assumptions for a Simulation of the Urban Residential Housing and Land Market* (Philadelphia: University of Pennsylvania Press, 1966).

36. Forrester, *op. cit.* (1961).

37. Forrester, *op. cit.* (1969), p. 14.

38. Forrester, *op. cit.* (1971).

39. Kan Chen, *et al.,* "Industrial Systems Modeling—I" (University of Pittsburgh, School of Engineering, April 1971), mimeographed.

40. L.P. Kadanaff, J.R. Voss, and W.J. Booknight, "A City Grows Before Your Eyes," *Computer Decisions,* Vol. 1, No. 3 (December 1969), pp. 16–23.

41. For a further discussion of the horizon planning model, *see* Alan Walter Steiss, *Public Budgeting and Management* (Lexington, Mass.: Lexington Books, D.C. Heath, 1972), chapter 9.

42. Anthony J. Catanese and Alan Walter Steiss, *Systemic Planning: Theory and Application* (Lexington, Mass.: Lexington Books, D.C. Heath, 1970).

43. Musil, *op. cit.,* p. 370.

Chapter 2
Theoretical Structure of the Model

1. Gunnar Myrdal, *An American Dilemma: The Negro Problem and Modern Democracy* (New York: Harper, 1944); *Asian Drama: An Inquiry into the Poverty of Nations,* Vol. III (New York: The Twentieth Century Fund, 1968).

2. Ragnar Nurske, *Problems of Capital Formation in Underdeveloped Countries* (Oxford: Basil Blackwell, 1953), p. 3.

3. Gunnar Myrdal, *Asian Drama: An Inquiry into the Poverty of Nations,* III (New York: The Twentieth Century Fund, 1968), p. 1844.

4. Eugene Staley, *The Future of Underdeveloped Countries* (New York: Harper, 1954), p. 13.

5. Lyle W. Shannon, *Underdeveloped Areas* (New York: Harper, 1957), pp. 1–2.

6. Norman S. Buchanan and Howard S. Ellis, *Approaches to Economic Development* (New York: The Twentieth Century Fund, 1955), pp. 3–4.

7. Myrdal, *op. cit.* (1968), p. 1846.

8. *Ibid.,* p. 1857.

9. W. Ross Ashby, *An Introduction to Cybernetics* (New York: John Wiley and Sons, 1963), p. 81.

10. Myrdal, *op. cit.* (1968), pp. 1871–78.

11. Jay W. Forrester, *Urban Dynamics* (Cambridge: MIT Press, 1969), pp. 13–14.

12. Jay W. Forrester, *Principles of Systems* (Cambridge: Wright-Allen, 1972), pp. 2–21.
13. Myrdal, *op. cit.* (1968), p. 1875.
14. Kimball Young, *Social Psychology* (New York: Appleton-Century-Crofts, 1956), p. 189.
15. *Ibid.*
16. Myrdal, *op. cit.* (1968), pp. 1876–78.
17. *Ibid.*, p. 1871.
18. F. Stuart Chapin, Jr., *Urban Land Use Planning* (Urbana: University of Illinois Press, 1970), pp. 29–39.

Chapter 3
The Study Area and Model Equations

1. Dade County Model City Agency, *Dade County Model City Program: Third Action Year* (Miami: Dade County, 1972), pp. 20–23.
2. *Ibid.*, pp. 22–25
3. *Ibid.*, pp. 15–20.
4. Simpson and Curtin, Transportation Engineers, *Model Cities Transit Program* (Miami, mimeographed, 1972), pp. i–ii.
5. Jay W. Forrester, *Urban Dynamics* (Cambridge: M.I.T. Press, 1969), p. 14.
6. James Coleman, *Equality of Educational Opportunity* (Washington: Government Printing Office, 1966), p. 312.
7. *Ibid.*
8. David M. Gordon, *Problems in Political Economy: An Urban Perspective* (Lexington, Mass.: Lexington Books, D.C. Heath, 1971), p. 163
9. William Edward, Jr., "Classroom Size and the Human Equation," *School and Community*, Vol. 55, No. 2 (October 1968), pp. 26–27.
10. Alice V. Keliher, "Effective Learning and the Teacher Ratio," *The Educational Digest*, Vol. 32, No. 5 (January 1967), pp. 20–22.
11. Edward, *op. cit.*, pp. 27–28.
12. Keliher, *op. cit.*, p. 21.
13. Gordon, *loc. cit.*
14. George Taylor, "The Effectiveness of Using Non-Teaching Professionals in a Selected Senior High School," *Journal of Secondary Education*, Vol. 46, No. 1 (January 1971), p. 64.
15. *Ibid.*, p. 65.
16. *Ibid.*, pp. 65–66.
17. Edward, *loc. cit.*
18. Coleman, *op. cit.*, pp. 317–18.
19. *Ibid.*, p. 317.
20. *Ibid.*, pp. 316–18.
21. *Ibid.*, pp. 314–15.
22. *Ibid.*, p. 302.

23. *Ibid.*, pp. 302–10.

24. Bennett Harrison, "Education and Underemployment in the Urban Ghetto," *op. cit.*, p. 185.

25. Coleman, *op. cit.*, pp. 320–21.

26. *Ibid.*

27. *Ibid.*, p. 321.

28. *Ibid.*, p. 320.

29. Robert Zito and Jack Bardon, "Negro Adolescent's Success and Failure Imagery Concerning Work and School," *The Vocational Guidance Quarterly*, Vol. 16, No. 3 (March 1968), pp. 181–84.

30. Gunnar Myrdal, *Asian Drama: An Inquiry into the Poverty of Nations*, III (New York: The Twentieth Century Fund, 1968), p. 1913.

31. Joel J. Albert, John Kosa, and Robert J. Haggerty, "A Month of Illness and Health Care Among Low-Income Families," *Public Health Reports*, Vol. 82, No. 8 (August 1967), p. 707.

32. Derek Robinson, "Use of Medical Services and Facilities by Welfare-Supported Children," *American Journal of Public Health*, Vol. 80, No. 12 (December 1965), p. 2282; Arthur J. Salisbury and Robert Berg, "Health Defects and Need for Treatment of Adolescents in Low Income Families," *Public Health Reports*, Vol. 84, No. 8 (August 1969), p. 710; Joyce C. Lashof, "Medical Care in the Urban Center," in Gordon, *op. cit.*, pp. 323–26.

33. Salisbiry, *loc. cit.*

34. Robinson, *loc. cit.*

35. Daniel M. Wilner, *et al.*, "Housing as an Environmental Factor in Mental Health: The Johns Hopkins Longitudinal Study," *American Journal of Public Health*, Vol. 50, No. 1 (January 1960), p. 65.

36. Michael D. Lebowitz and James C. Malcolm, "Socioeconomic Analysis of the Alameda County Health Department Jurisdiction," *American Journal of Public Health*, Vol. 54, No. 11 (November 1964), pp. 1876–81; Jean E. Bedger, "Socioeconomic Characteristics in Relation to Maternal and Child Health," *Public Health Reports*, Vol. 81, No. 9 (September 1966), p. 832.

37. Wilner, *op. cit.*, pp. 55–63.

38. Serena E. Wade, "Trends in Public Knowledge About Health and Illness," *American Journal of Public Health*, Vol. 60, No. 3 (March 1970), p. 488.

39. Barbara O. Henkel, *Community Health* (Boston: Allyn & Bacon, 1970), pp. 327–48.

40. Gary S. Becker, *The Economics of Discrimination* (Chicago: University of Chicago Press, 1957), pp. 111–12; Larry D. Singell, "Barriers to Earning Income," *Quarterly Review of Economica and Business*, Vol. 8, No. 2 (September 1968), p. 40; John Parker and Louis B. Shaw, "Labor Force Participation Within Metropolitan Areas," *Southern Economic Journal*, Vol. 34, No. 4 (April 1968), p. 542.

41. Harrison, *op. cit.*, pp. 181–90.

42. Albert, *et al.*, *loc. cit.*

43. Becker, *op. cit.*, pp. 113–14.
44. James Gwartney, "Changes in the Nonwhite/White Income Ratio–1937–67," *American Economic Review,* Vol. 60, No. 5 (December 1970), pp. 872–83.
45. Herbert R. Northrup and Richard L. Rowan (eds.), *The Negro and Employment Opportunity: Problems and Practices* (Ann Arbor: Bureau of Industrial Relations, University of Michigan, 1965).
46. Arthur M. Ross and Herbert Hill (eds.), *Employment, Race, and Poverty* (New York: Harcourt, Brace, 1967).
47. Singell, *op. cit.*, p. 38.
48. *Ibid.*, p. 39.

Chapter 4
Model Simulation and Projections

1. Gunnar Myrdal, *Asian Drama: An Inquiry into the Poverty of Nations,* III (New York: The Twentieth Century Fund, 1968), pp. 1944–46.
2. Larry D. Singell, "Barriers to Earning Income," *Quarterly Review of Economics and Business,* Vol. 8, No. 2 (September 1968).
3. Gary S. Becker, *The Economics of Discrimination* (Chicago: University of Chicago Press, 1957).
4. Myrdal, *op. cit.*, pp. 1859–1940.
5. Simpson and Curtin, Transportation Engineers, *Model Cities Transit Program* (Miami, mimeographed, 1972).
6. James Coleman, *Equality of Educational Opportunity* (Washington, D.C.: Government Printing Office, 1966), pp. 39–43.
7. Arthur J. Salisbury and Robert Berg, "Health Defects and Need for Treatment of Adolescents in Low Income Families," *Public Health Reports,* Vol. 84, No. 8 (August 1969); Derek Robinson, "Use of Medical Services and Facilities by Welfare-Supported Children," *American Journal of Public Health,* Vol. 80, No. 12 (December 1965).
8. Allen Hodges and Herbert Dorkin, "Location and Outpatient Psychiatric Care," *Public Health REports,* Vol. 76, No. 3 (March 1961), pp. 239–41; Jerome W. Lubin, *et al.,* "Highway Network Minimum Path Selection Applied to Health Facility Planning," *Public Health Reports,* Vol. 80, No. 9 (September 1965), pp. 771–78.
9. William L. Garrison, *et al., Studies of Highway Development and Geographic Change* (Seattle: University of Washington Press, 1954), pp. 229–76.
10. *Ibid.*, p. 231.
11. As cited by Charles Goetz, Department of Economics, Virginia Polytechnic Institute and State University, in discussion of the present work, August 22, 1972.

Chapter 5
Sensitivity Analysis

1. Ira S. Lowry, "A Short Course in Model Design," in *Spatial Analysis: A Reader in Statistical Geography*, edited by Brian J. Berry and Duane F. Marble (Englewood Cliffs, 1968), pp. 53–64.
2. Gunnar Myrdal, *Asian Drama: An Inquiry into the Poverty of Nations*, III (New York: The Twentieth Century Fund, 1968), pp. 1873–78.
3. Alan Walter Steiss, *Public Budgeting and Management* (Lexington, Mass: Lexington Books, D.C. Heath, 1972), p. 136.

Chapter 6
Conclusions, Model Evaluation, Future Research

1. Donella Meadows, *et al.*, *Limits to Growth* (New York: Signet, 1972); Jay W. Forrester, *Urban Dynamics* (Cambridge: MIT Press, 1969).
2. Gunnar Myrdal, *Asian Drama: An Inquiry into the Poverty of Nations*, III (New York: The Twentieth Century Fund, 1968), p. 1846.
3. *Ibid.*, p. 1857.
4. Forrester, *op. cit.*, pp. 227–49.
5. Roger L. Creighton, *Urban Transportation Planning* (Urbana: University of Illinois Press, 1970), pp. 193–212.
6. John W. Dickey, "Mimimizing Economic Segregation Through Transit System Changes: A Goal Programming Approach," in *Traffic Flow and Transportation*, edited by Gorden F. Newell (New York: American Elsevier, 1972), pp. 87–108.
7. Jay W. Forrester, *Principles of Systems* (Cambridge, Mass.: Wright-Allen Press, 1972), pp. 5–10.

Bibliography

Albert, Joel J., *et al.* "A Month of Illness and Health Care Among Low-Income Families." *Public Health Reports.* Vol. 82, No. 8. (August 1967), pp. 705–13.

Baali, Fuad, and Joseph S. Vandiver (eds.). *Urban Sociology: Contemporary Readings.* New York: Appleton-Century-Crofts, 1970.

Bain, Joe S. *Pricing, Distribution, and Employment: Economics of an Enterprise System.* New York: Holt, 1948.

Baldwin, Robert E. *Economic Development and Growth.* 2nd. ed. New York: John Wiley & Sons, 1972.

Bartos, Otomar J. *Simple Models of Group Behavior.* New York: Columbia University Press, 1967.

Becker, Gary S. *The Economics of Discrimination.* 2nd ed. Chicago: University of Chicago Press, 1971.

Bedger, Jean E. "Socioeconomic Characteristics in Relation to Maternal and Child Care," *Public Health Reports.* Vol. 81, No. 9. (September 1966), pp. 829–33.

Bensusan-Butt, David M. *On Economic Growth.* London: Oxford University Press, 1960.

Bergstrom, A.R. *Selected Economic Models and Their Analysis.* New York: American Elsevier, 1967.

Berry, Brian J.L., and Frank E. Horton. *Geographic Perspectives on Urban Systems: With Integrated Readings.* Englewood Cliffs: Prentice-Hall, Inc., 1970.

Berry, Brian J.L., and Duane Marble (eds.). *Spatial Analysis: A Reader in Statistical Geography.* Englewood Cliffs: Prentice-Hall, 1968.

Bowen, William, and T. Aldrich Finnegan. "Educational Attainment and Labor Force Participation," *American Economic Review,* Vol. 56, No. 2. (May 1966), pp. 567–82.

Brown, T. Merritt. *Specification and Uses of Econometric Models.* London: Macmillan, 1970.

Brimmer, Andrew F. "Education and the Economic Advancement of Minority Groups," *Integrated Education: Race and Schools.* Vol. 8, No. 2 (March–April 1970), pp. 48–55.

Carney, David. *Patterns and Mechanics of Economic Growth: A General Theoretical Approach.* Antioch: The Antioch Press, 1967.

Cauffman, Joy G., *et al.* "Health Care of School Children: Variations Among Ethnic Groups," *The Journal of School Health,* Vol. 39, No. 5 (May 1969), pp. 296–304.

Chapin, F. Stuart, Jr. *Urban Land Use Planning.* 2nd ed. Urbana: University of
    Illinois Press, 1970.

Chiang, Alpha C. *Fundamental Methods of Mathematical Economics.* New York:
    McGraw-Hill, 1967.

Chisholm, Michael, *et al. Regional Forecasting.* London: Betterworths, 1971.

Chu, Kong. *Principles of Econometrics.* Scranton: International Textbook
    Company, 1968.

Cole, William E. *Urban Society: A College Textbook In Urban Sociology.*
    Boston: Houghton Mifflin, 1958.

Coleman, James, *Equality of Educational Opportunity.* Washington: Government
    Printing Office, 1966.

Committee For Economic Development. *Raising Low Incomes through Improved
    Education.* New York: Committee For Economic Development, September
    1965.

Coons, Alvin E. *The Income of Nations and Persons: An Introduction to
    Economics.* Chicago: Rand McNally, 1959.

Cramer, J.S. *Empirical Econometrics.* Amsterdam: North-Holland Publishing
    Company, 1971.

Creighton, Roger L. *Urban Transportation Planning.* Urbana: University of
    Illinois Press, 1970.

Culbertson, John M. *Economc Development: An Ecological Approach.* New
    York: Knopf, 1971.

Dade County Model City Agency. *Dade County Model City Program: Third
    Action Year Plan.* Miami: Dade County, 1972.

Daugherty, Marion. *Understanding Economic Growth.* Atlanta: Scott, Foresman,
    1961.

Dickey, John W., and R.A. Hall. "Experiments with an Interactive Search Pro-
    cedure for Changing Transportation to Guide Urban Growth," Civil
    Engineering Department, V.P.I. & S.U., 1971. Mimeographed.

Dickey, John, Phillip Leone, and Alan Schwarte. "Use of TOPAZ for Generating
    Alternate Land Use Schemes." Unpublished manuscript, Virginia Poly-
    technic Institute. Division of Environmental and Urban Systems, 1971.

Duhl, Leonard J. (ed.). *The Urban Condition: People and Policy in the Metropolis.*
    New York: Basic Books, 1963.

Durr, Fred. *The Urban Economy.* Scranton: Intext Educational Publishers, 1971.

Edward, Williams, Jr. "Classroom Size and the Human Equation," *School and
    Community,* Vol. 55, No. 2 (October 1968), pp. 26–30.

Engle, Arthur. *Perspective in Health Planning.* London: University of London
    Athlone Press, 1968.

Feldman, Jacob J. *The Dissemination of Health Information: A Case Study in
    Adult Learning.* Chicago: Aldine Publishing Company, 1966.

Fillmer, Henry T., and Helen S. Kahn. "Race, Socio-economic Level, Housing,
    and Reading Readiness." *The Reading Teacher,* Vol. 21, No. 2 (November
    1967), pp. 153–57.

Forrester, Jay W. *Industrial Dynamics.* Published jointly. Cambridge: M.I.T. Press;
    New York: John Wiley & Sons, 1961.

——. *Principles of Systems.* Cambridge, Mass: Wright-Allen Press, 1972.

——. *Urban Dynamics.* Cambridge: M.I.T. Press, 1969.

Furtado, Celso. *Development and Underdevelopment.* Translated by Ricardo De Aguiar and Enc C. Drysdale. Berkeley: University of California Press, 1964.

Garrison, William, *et al. Studies of Highway Development and Geographic Change.* Seattle: University of Washington Press, 1959.

Gordon, David M. (ed.). Problems in Political Economy. *An Urban Perspective.* Lexington, Mass. D.C. Heath, 1971.

Gornick, Marian E., *et al.* "Use of Medical Services as Demanded by the Urban Poor," *American Journal of Public Health,* Vol. 50, (August 1969), pp. 1302–11.

Greenhut, Melvin L., and Frank H. Jackson. *Intermediate Income and Growth Theory.* Englewood Cliffs: Prentice-Hall, 1961.

Gwartney, James. "Changes in the Nonwhite/White Income Ratio—1939–67," *American Economic Review,* Vol. 60, No. 5 (December 1970), pp. 872–83.

Hagen, Evertt E. *The Economics of Development.* Homewood: Richard D. Irwin, 1968.

Haggett, Peter. *Locational Analysis in Human Geography.* London: Edward Arnold, 1965.

Hamberg, Daniel. *Models of Economic Growth.* New York: Harper, 1971.

Hanlon, John J. *Principles at Public Health Administration.* 5th ed. Saint Louis: C.V. Mosby, 1969.

Haring, Joseph E. (ed.). *Urban and Regional Economics: Perspectives for Public Action.* Boston: Houghton Mifflin, 1972.

Henderson, Edmund H., and Barbara H. Long. "Correlations of Reading Readiness Among Children of Varying Background," *Reading Teacher,* Vol. 22, No. 1 (October 1968), pp. 40–44.

Henderson, William L., and Larry C. Lebebur. *Urban Economics: Processes and Problems.* New York: John Wiley & Sons, 1972.

Henkel, Barbara Osborn. *Community Health.* 2nd ed. Boston: Allyn & Bacon, 1970.

Hill, Charles. "Teachers as Change Agents," *The Clearing House,* Vol. 45, No. 7 (March 1971), pp. 424–28.

Hirsch, Jay, and Joan Costello. "School Achievers and Underachievers in an Urban Ghetto," *The Elementary School Journal,* Vol. 71, No. 2 (November 1970), pp. 78–85.

Hill, Kennedy, and Jerome B. Dusek. "Children's Achievement Expectations As a Function of Social Reinforcement, Sex of S, and Test Anxiety," *Child Development,* Vol. 40, No. 2 (June 1969), pp. 547–49.

Hobson, W. (ed.). *The Theory and Practice of Public Health.* 3rd. ed. London: Oxford University Press, 1969.

Hodges, Allen, and Herbert Dorken. "Location and Outpatient Psychiatric Care," *Public Health Reports,* Vol. 76, No. 3 (March 1961), p. 239.

Hoover, Kenneth H., Victor H. Baumann, and Susanne M. Schafer. "The Influence of Class-Size Variations on Cognitive and Affective Learning of College Freshmen," *The Journal of Experimental Education,* Vol. 38, No. 3 (Spring 1970), pp. 30–43.

Hopkins, Edward Scott. *et al.* (eds.). *The Practice of Sanitation: in Its Relation to the Environment.* 4th ed. Baltimore: Williams & Wilkins, 1970.

Horowitz, David. *The Abolition of Poverty.* New York: Praeger Publishers, 1969.

Jaszi, Helen H. (ed.). *Empirical Studies in Health Economics: Proceedings of the Second Conference on the Economics of Health.* Baltimore: Johns Hopkins Press, 1970.

Joiner, Lee M. "Socioeconomic Status and Perceived Expectations As Measures of Family Influence," *Personnel and Guidance Journal,* Vol. 47, No. 7 (March 1969), pp. 655–59.

Katz, Fred E. (ed.). *Contemporary Sociological Theory.* New York: Random House, 1971.

Keliher, Alice V. "Effective Learning and the Teacher Pupil Ratio," *The Educational Digest,* Vol. 32, No. 5 (January 1967), pp. 20–22.

Kibel, Barry M. *Simulation of the Urban Environment.* Washington: Association of American Geographers, 1972.

Kogan, Benjamin A. (ed.). *Readings in Health Science.* New York: Harcourt Brace Jovanovich, 1971.

Kohl, Herbert. *36 Children.* New York: New American Library, 1967.

Kosa, John, *et al.* (eds.) *Poverty and Health: A Sociological Analysis.* Cambridge: Harvard University Press, 1969.

Kozol, Jonathan. *Death At an Early Age: The Destruction of the Hearts and Minds of Negro Children in the Boston Public Schools.* Boston: Houghton Mifflin, 1967.

Lebowitz, Michael D., and James C. Malcolm. "Socioeconomic Analysis of the Alameda County Health Department Jurisdiction," *American Journal of Public Health,* Vol. 54, No. 11 (November 1964), pp. 1876–81.

Loewenstein, Louis K. (ed.). *Urban Studies: An Introductory Reader.* New York: The Free Press, 1971.

Lubin, Jerome, *et al.* "Highway Minimum Path Selection Applied to Health Facility Planning," *Public Health Reports.* Vol. 80, No. 9 (September 1965), pp. 771–78.

Lurie, Melvin, and Elton Rayack. "Employment Opportunities for Negro Families in Satellite Cities," *Southern Economic Journal,* Vol. 36, No. 2 (October 1969), pp. 191–95.

Machlup, Fritz. *Education and Economic Growth.* Lincoln: University of Nebraska Press, 1970.

Mackler, Bernard. "Blacks Who Are Academically Successful," *Urban Education,* Vol. 5, No. 1 (April 1970), pp. 210–37.

Meadows, Donella, *et al. Limits to Growth.* New York: Signet, 1972.

Mehta, F.K. *Economics of Growth.* 2nd ed. revised and enlarged. London: Asia Publishing House, 1970.

Meyer, John R. (ed.). *Techniques of Transport Planning.* Vol. II: *Systems Analysis and Simulation Models* by David T. Kresge and Paul O. Roberts. Washington, D.C.: The Brookings Institution, Transport Research Program, 1971.

Morgan, James, and David Martin. "Education and Income," *Quarterly Journal of Economics,* Vol. 67, No. 3 (August 1963), pp. 423–37.

Myrdal, Gunnar. *An American Dilemma: The Negro Problem and Modern Democracy.* New York: Harper, 1944.

——. *Asian Drama: An Inquiry Into the Poverty of Nations.* New York: The Twentieth Century Fund, 1968.

——. *The Challenge of World Poverty: A World Anti-Poverty Program in Outline.* New York: Pantheon, 1970.

Netzer, Dick. *Economics and Urban Problems: Diagnoses and Prescriptions.* New York: Basic Books, 1970.

Newell, Gordon F. *Traffic Flow and Transportation:* Proceedings of the Fifth International Symposium on the Theory of Traffic Flow and Transportation. New York: American Elsevier, 1972.

Northrup, Herbert R., and Richard L. Rowan (eds.). *The Negro and Employment Opportunity: Problems and Practices.* Ann Arbor: Bureau of Industrial Relations, Graduate School of Business Administration, The University of Michigan, 1965.

Nurske, Ragnar. *Problems of Capital Formation in Underdeveloped Countries.* Oxford: Basil Blackwell, 1953.

Parker, John E., and Lois B. Shaw. "Labor Force Participation Within Metropolitan Areas," *Southern Economic Journal,* Vol. 34, No. 4 (April 1968), pp. 538–47.

Perloff, Harvey S., and Lowdon Wingo, Jr. (eds.). *Issues in Urban Economics.* Baltimore: The Johns Hopkins Press, 1968.

Perloff, Harvey. "Problems of Raising Incomes in Lagging Sectors of the Economy," *American Economic Review,* Vol. 50, No. 2 (May 1960), pp. 223–30.

Pugh, Alexander. *Dynamo II Users Manual.* 3rd ed. Cambridge: M.I.T. Press, 1971.

Robinson, Derek. "Use of Medical Services and Facilities by Welfare-Supported Children," *American Journal of Public Health,* Vol. 80 (December 1965), pp. 2280–85.

Ross, Arthur M., and Herbert Hill (eds.). *Employment, Race, and Poverty.* New York: Harcourt, Brace, 1967.

Salisburg, Arthur J., and Robert Berg. "Health Defects and Need for Treatment of Adolescents in Low Income Families," *Public Health Reports,* Vol. 84, No. 8 (August 1969), pp. 705–11.

Samuelson, Paul A. *Economics: An Introductory Analysis.* 4th ed. New York: McGraw-Hill, 1958.

Schuchter, Arnold. *White Power/Black Freedom: Planning the Future of Urban America.* Boston: Beacon Press, 1968.

Sexton, Patricia C. *Education and Income: Inequalities of Opportunity in Our Public Schools.* New York: Viking, 1961.

Simpson and Curtin, Transportation Engineers, *Model Cities Transit Program.* Miami 1962.

Singell, Larry D. "Barriers to Earning Income," *Quarterly Review of Economics and Business,* Vol. 8, No. 2 (September 1968), pp. 35–44.

Smelser, Neil J., and James A. Davis (eds.). *Sociology.* Englewood Cliffs: Prentice-Hall, 1969.

Smolensky, Jack, and Franklin Haar. *Principles of Community Health.* 2nd ed. Philadelphia: W.B. Saunders, 1967.

Sorkin, Alan L. "Education, Migration and Negro Unemployment," *Social Forces,* Vol. 47, No. 3 (March 1969), pp. 265–74.

Snyder, Eleanor. "Low Income in Urban Areas," *American Economic Review,* Vol. 80, No. 2 (May 1960), pp. 243–50.

Spiegelglas, Stephen, and Charles J. Welsh (eds.). *Economic Development: Challenge and Promise.* Englewood Cliffs: Prentice-Hall, 1970.

Taylor, George. "The Effects of Using Non-Teaching Professionals in a Selected Senior High School," *Journal of Secondary Education,* Vol. 46, No. 1 (January 1971), pp. 60–67.

Thompson, Wilbur R. *A Preface to Urban Economics.* Baltimore: The Johns Hopkins Press, 1965.

Tucker, Murray. "Effect of Heavy Medical Expenditures on Low-Income Families," *Public Health Reports.* Vol. 85, No. 5 (May 1970), pp. 419–25.

U.S. Department of Commerce. Bureau of the Census. *1970 Census of Population and Housing: Census Tracts: Miami, Florida. Standard Metropolitan Statistical Area.*

Wade, Serena E. "Trends in Public Knowledge About Health and Illness," *American Journal of Public Health,* Vol. 63, No. 3 (March 1970), pp. 485–91.

Weeks, H. Ashley. *Family Spending Patterns and Health Care.* Cambridge: Harvard University Press, 1961.

Weinberg, S. Kirson. *Social Problems in Modern Urban Society.* 2nd ed. Englewood Cliffs: Prentice-Hall, 1970.

Wilner, Daniel M., *et al.* "Housing as an Environmental Factor in Mental Health: The Johns Hopkins Longitudinal Study," *American Journal of Public Health,* Vol. 50, No. 1, (January 1960), pp. 55–63.

Zito, Robert, and Jack Bardon. "Negro Adolescent's Success and Failure Imagery Concerning Work and School," *The Vocational Guidance Quarterly,* Vol. 16, No. 3 (March 1968), pp. 181–84.

Author Index

Subject Index

About the Authors

Alan Walter Steiss is Associate Dean for Research and Public Service of the College of Architecture and Urban Studies, Virginia Polytechnic Institute and State University. A graduate of Bucknell University (A.B. in Psychology and Sociology) and the University of Wisconsin (M.A. and Ph.D. in Urban and Regional Planning), Dr. Steiss has served at Virginia Tech as Director of the Center for Urban and Regional Studies, Chairman of Urban and Regional Planning and Urban Affairs, and Chairman of the Division of Environmental and Urban Systems. He has been a guest lecturer at several universities, including Rider College, New York University, the University of Wisconsin, Georgia Institute of Technology, Virginia Commonwealth University, and the University of British Columbia. Formerly the head of statewide planning for the State of New Jersey, he has served as a consultant to the states of Wisconsin, New Jersey, Maryland, Virginia, South Carolina, New York, and Hawaii, and the Trust Territory of the Pacific. Dr. Steiss is the author of several books, including *Planning Administration; A Framework for Planning in State Government; Systemic Planning: Theory and Application* (with Anthony J. Catanese); *A Public Service Option for Architectural Curricula; Public Budgeting and Management; Models for the Analysis and Planning of Urban Systems;* and *Urban Systems Dynamics.* He has contributed to numerous professional journals in the United States and abroad.

John W. Dickey is Associate Professor and Director of the Center for Urban and Regional Studies at Virginia Polytechnic Institute and State University. He received the B.S.C.E. from Lehigh University and the Ph.D. in civil engineering (transportation) from Northwestern University. Dr. Dickey is on several regional, state, and national transportation committees and task forces and has done urban systems research in India and Australia. His primary teaching and research interests include transportation planning, urban systems methodology, land use modelling, land use allocation in urban areas, interactive processes between planner and decision-makers, implementation strategies, and urban performance indicators. Dr. Dickey is coauthor (with David M. Glancy and Ernest M. Jennelle) of *Technology Assessment* (Lexington Books, 1973). His other books include *Metropolitan Transportation Planning, TOPAZ: Planning Technique and Applications,* and *Urban Systems Research.*

Bruce Phelps is the Transportation Coordinator of the Mid Willamette Valley Council of Governments in Salem, Oregon. A graduate of San Francisco State College, the University of California at Berkeley, and Virginia Polytechnic Institute and State University, Mr. Phelps has worked in the federal government as a geographer and in planning as both a water quality management planner and a transportation planner. He has taught environmental planning at Virginia Polytechnic Institute, New River Community College in Virginia, and Chemeketa Community College in Oregon. The views in this book do not necessarily represent those of the Mid Willamette Valley Council of Governments.

Michael W. Harvey is Staff Associate–Current Planning at the Chesapeake and Potomac Telephone Company of Virginia. His responsibilities encompass the coordination of capital budgeting and short-range local exchange planning. Educated at Virginia Polytechnic Institute and State University, he is an associate member of the American Institute of Planners and a member of the American Society of Planning Officials. He is a coauthor of "Community," a community development simulation game published in 1972 by the Virginia Polytechnic Institute and State University Extension Division.